The Guardian

CRYPTIC CROSSWORDS BOOK 2

T0118263

Published in 2022 by Welbeck
an imprint of Welbeck Non-Fiction,
part of Welbeck Publishing Group
Based in London and Sydney
www.welbeckpublishing.com

Text and Puzzles © 2022 Guardian News & Media Limited
Design © 2022 Welbeck Non-Fiction,
part of Welbeck Publishing Group

Editorial: Ben McConnell and Millie Acers
Design: Bauer Media and Eliana Holder

All rights reserved. No part of this publication may be
reproduced, stored in a retrieval system, or transmitted
in any form or by any means, electronically, mechanical,
photocopying, recording or otherwise, without the prior
permission of the copyright owners and the publishers.

A CIP catalogue for this book is available from the British
Library.

ISBN: 978-1-80279-104-4

Printed in the United Kingdom

10 9 8 7 6 5 4 3 2 1

The Guardian

CRYPTIC CROSSWORDS ^{BOOK} 2

A compendium of more than **100** difficult puzzles

WELBECK

About the Guardian

The *Guardian* has published honest and fearless journalism, free from commercial or political interference, since it was founded in 1821.

It now also publishes a huge variety of puzzles every day, both online and in print, covering many different types of crosswords, sudoku, general knowledge quizzes and more.

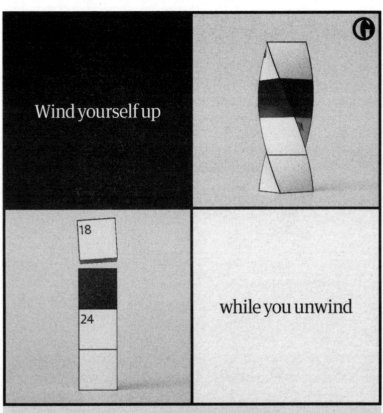

Wind yourself up

while you unwind

Get that "punch the air" feeling. Download the Guardian Puzzles app and challenge yourself with more than 15,000 crosswords and sudokus, from easy to infuriating.

Search "Guardian Puzzles" in the App Store or Google Play.

The GuardianPuzzles

Introduction

Welcome to the second book in the *Guardian*'s brain-teasing puzzle series. The cryptic crossword puzzle has appeared in the pages of the *Guardian* for nearly a century, and these crosswords have been curated especially from recent issues to form a bumper batch of pure enjoyment.

Cryptic crosswords are one of the most perplexing puzzle types there are, but as a consequence they are also one of the most pleasing to solve. You will need linguistic skills, lateral-thinking abilities and plenty of patience to complete this book. The compilers have provided just enough clever clues to lead you to the right answer, but it will almost certainly take you some time to get there.

Above all though, please enjoy this book! The world is full of challenges, but we hope that these challenges will provide a delightful diversion for you.

Set by Puck

ACROSS

1,4 Empty nest and no memories — bad time for OAP? (6,6)

9 As part of time-sharing, taking turn in house (4)

10 Horrify a mate, forgetting name for mountain area (10)

11 Pensioner cycling by checkpoint made from shoddy material (6)

12 Out of power, allowed to be smutty? (8)

13 Rest of Italian team's smutty, reportedly (9)

15 Tory wearing light blue (4)

16 A Christian GP, say, covering 10 (4)

17 Remote possibility of bad luck (3,6)

21 One performing unprepared, left holding a hole-boring tool? On the contrary (2-6)

22 Definitely happening — keep waiting to be connected (2,4)

24 Abundance of fast sex between dessert and coffee, ultimately (10)

25 Sign new back for present season (4)

26,27 Photographic chemical uncovering magic (6,6)

DOWN

1,16 Joyce's alter ego, in phase with male name ("boy raised in God") (7,7)

2 Writing up article about show in African capital (5)

3 Having prolonged good luck, film here once? (2,1,4)

5 Kiss one of two kissers wearing very large bloomers (6)

6 Woman with adopted youngster eating a Mexican dish (9)

7,19 Reticently, I log off site that's educational (7,7)

8 Fantastically fine and super, so extremely delightful? (13)

14 Moving in Puck's direction, turned up on island, then left (9)

16 See 1

18 On the point of cupboard love (5,2)

19 See 7

20 Make former pupil tell story about the origin of greed (6)

23 Language coming from noisy party after stripper's act (5)

Solution see page 249

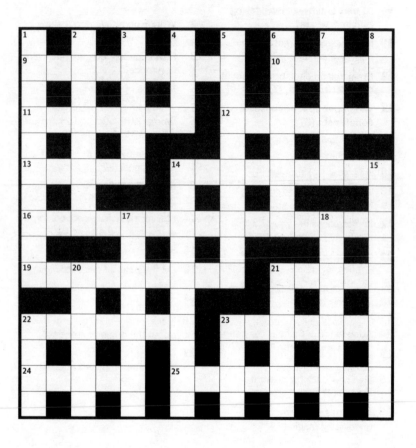

ACROSS

9 Masses of hot oil sprinkled twice over river (3,6)

10 Literary Dick, one in a black suit (5)

11 Music paper accompanying magazine (7)

12 Greek region once booted out rival every so often (7)

13 Wide open space in hospital department (5)

14 Land in the saddle? That's Turpin's job (7,2)

16 It galls terribly to smell book that I can't grasp (3,3,5,2,2)

19 With which to see stars become smaller (9)

21 Authority keeps quiet (3-2)

22 Expert writer's record collection (7)

23 Gap in head painlessly fixed, I'll set out (7)

24 Wear black uniform during early hours (5)

25 Father abandons French car carrying one dish (9)

DOWN

1 Drug dealer and pacifist? Not if nursing wound (10)

2 Plans day writing about one Asian city (8)

3 What's applied during period in ER (6)

4 Plant on its own, name missing (4)

5 What infidels do beside evil rebels (10)

6 Ringmaster is keen to employ star (8)

7 Scruffy artillerymen joke about origin of tanks (6)

8 It's on board primarily for everyone to appreciate (4)

14 He got merry playing instrument in greenhouse, maybe (10)

15 Amazing chap with Roman name visits friend (10)

17 Paisley goes in to bless worried Aegean islanders (8)

18 Godlike, round, soft-spoken Scotsman (8)

20 Where Lucy did the twist with me? (6)

21 Indy's edited by Conservative business agent (6)

22 Expert goes over minutes for summit (4)

23 Cryptic concerning Shed faction (4)

Solution see page 249

ACROSS

8 Composer accepting billion pounds for percussion instrument (8)

9 Olive eaten by male astrophysicist (5)

10 Ecstasy and anger in Ireland (4)

11 Eccentric horologer with a wind problem (10)

12 After change of leader, several become exhausted (3,3)

14 Old ducks spell trouble for gastropod (3,5)

15 Our sort of environmentalists retired, overwhelmed by burden (3,2,2)

17 Cover skin of backside with trousers, back to front (7)

20 Creep round ridiculously cool green hotel (8)

22 Married prince leaving old Spanish capital for plateau (6)

23 Imposed order on society, yet missed vagrant (10)

24 Coarse group of women, rowdily discontented (4)

25 Prayer of thanks from good people (5)

26 Remains for ever in mind, we'll swear (8)

DOWN

1 Quiet historian losing footing on edges of ruin (8)

2 Slothful extremes of island life (4)

3 Maidens periodically need bluesy tunes (6)

4 Scientist loves squeezing large marrow (7)

5 Seniors righted a wrong (5,3)

6 Turns section of poultry farm into co-op? (10)

7 Arab in Italy supporting the old folk (6)

13 Roman emperor, regularly ignoring advisor, called time on Scotsman (10)

16 Mum dined merrily, as luminous as ever (8)

18 All children tire, lying about (8)

19 Dramatic deep breaths heard over microphone (7)

21 Iroquois dude turned up in California area (6)

22 Girl said medic mostly managed (4,2)

24 Roots of sow thistle are dedicated gardener's enemy (4)

Solution see page 249

4 Set by Arachne

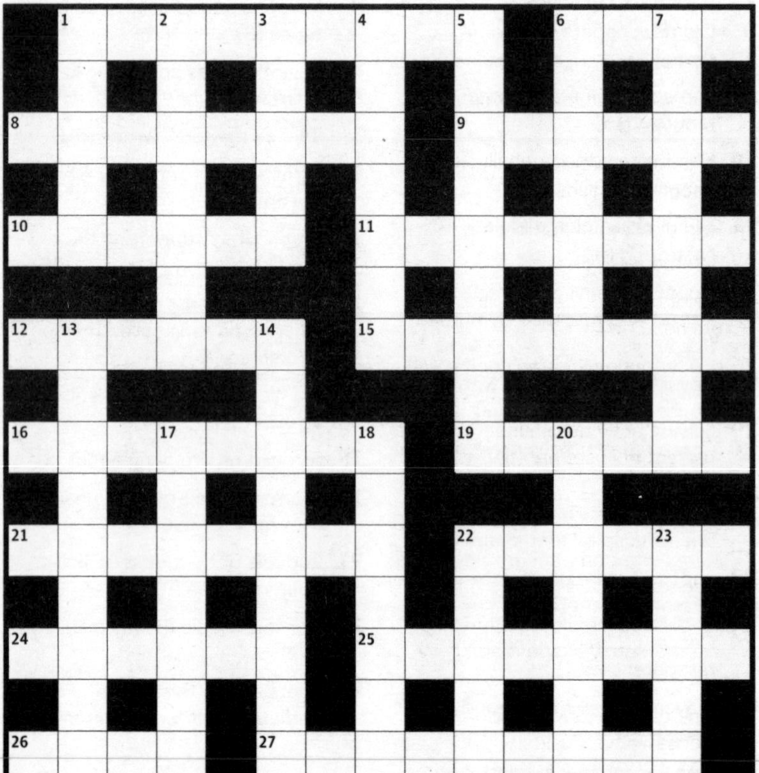

ACROSS

1 Rogue caught mate dividing loot (9)

6 Young setter, perhaps a future monarch? (4)

8 Old newspapers, frequently dated (8)

9 Romeo donning skimpy garment for crowd (6)

10 Flaming row, theoretically about increase in GDP (6)

11 Skilfully manipulate idolatry (8)

12 Infamous Clyde pub brawl (6)

15 Paint big birds seizing big cat by its head (8)

16 Party touring Russian capital heading off to share bed (6,2)

19 Leisure activities shunned by current philosopher (6)

21 Individual from Naples — or Barking? (8)

22 City centre emptied after I came, according to Caesar (6)

24 Rebellious female with gun unfortunately suspended again (6)

25 One of twelve sworn to follow Conservative illusionist (8)

26 Skinned bits ache and burn (4)

27 Game of cricket put strain on marriage (4,5)

DOWN

1 Close to terror under settee, until now (2,3)

2 Revolutionary Red regularly tilting at pacifist (4-3)

3 Poorly MP hesitantly collecting bodily fluid (5)

4 Dissipation of American male covered by the Guardian (7)

5 Vacuous government accepts zero-hour contract ought to pass (2,7)

6 A thousand and one transfixing openings for tales (7)

7 Pole dancer almost breaking laws (5,4)

13 Reparations united people over time (9)

14 Diminutive Man Friday's last few hours? (9)

17 Hum bits, playing heavy metal (7)

18 Dad does up opulent houses (7)

20 Mum disheartened after earl leaves beanfeast (7)

22 MI5 served up poison (5)

23 Idiot husband in Paisley? (5)

Solution see page 250

5 Set by Vulcan

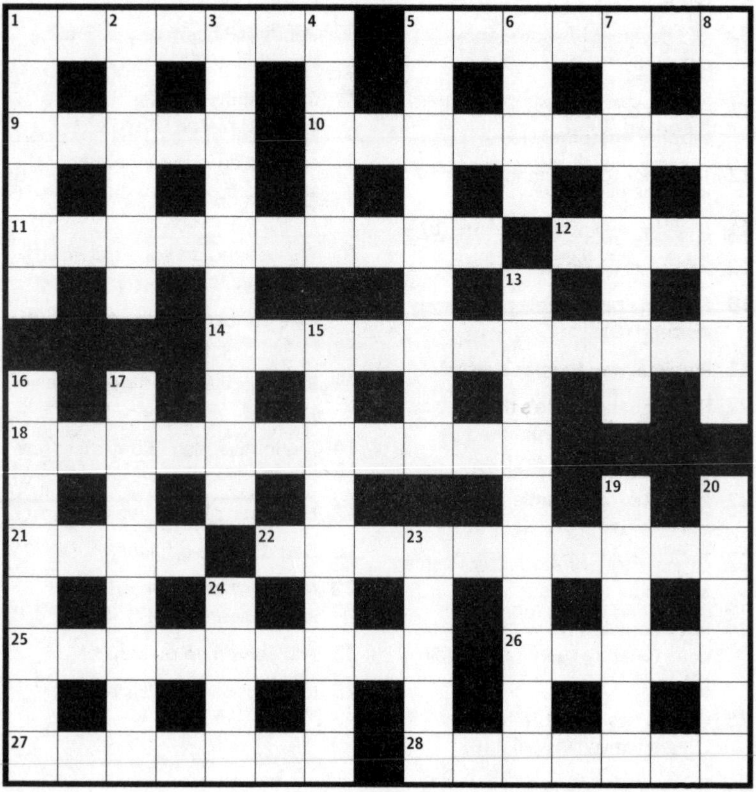

ACROSS

1 Drivers get through distance that's unnatural (7)

5 No peace till one's buried (7)

9 Melon, rotten fruit (5)

10 Board wanted to get you on board (9)

11 Her husband-to-be was a slippery customer (10)

12 Trunk not to be opened roughly (2,2)

14 Resolute mob rioting is vexatious (11)

18 Seeking computer technology is inviting trouble (6,3,2)

21 Precious way to start a letter (4)

22 Housecoat a stone's throw away? (10)

25 Weed, crushed, smells oddly (9)

26 Schoolteacher's random call? (5)

27 Showing no emotion over divine corpse (7)

28 Commend phone function to roam (7)

DOWN

1 Out of spite, start to malign girl (6)

2 Make one think again (6)

3 Competitor cannot broadcast about match (10)

4 Excellent performance on course for high-flyer (5)

5 Fragment of Messiah heard, part of a cycle (9)

6 Get a peep inside binder (4)

7 Top-level clearance (8)

8 Assume control of Special K and overeat (4,4)

13 Be sacked — and guillotined? (3,3,4)

15 Less popular time to be on shore, presumably, with boy (3,6)

16 Players got on, plastered (8)

17 Musical would be fine, if shortened (8)

19 Tries hard with a cereal (3,1,2)

20 Restrained? Cheats appallingly (6)

23 A block picked up is wood (5)

24 Very light haircut a bargain? (4)

Solution see page 250

Set by Chifonie

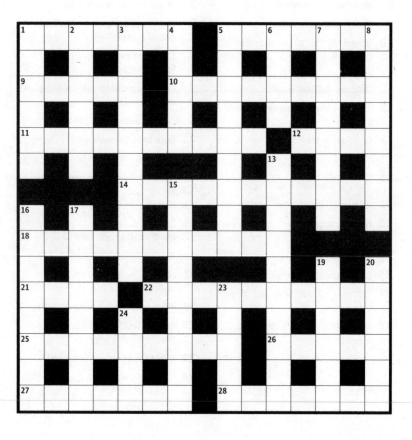

ACROSS

1 Eat away at fuel element in heart of reactor (7)

5 Judge a royal nipper (7)

9 Turner is delayed about an hour (5)

10 Theatre company dislike picture (9)

11 Open vessel journalist upset (10)

12 Greet bad weather (4)

14 Siren in car sent hens crazy (11)

18 Trendy Italian banker boxes celebrated doctor (11)

21 Look suggestively back in the dance (4)

22 Mrs Mopp has time to recycle liqueur (10)

25 Relative gets a halt signal that's not vindicated (9)

26 Children's game gets you and me in river (5)

27 Camera socket stolen by son with long-handled instrument (3,4)

28 Part of the creche longs for rank (7)

DOWN

1 Immature animal eats everything (6)

2 Cad runs over appealing carnivore (6)

3 Alien hiding in public dance is lacking restraint (4,3,3)

4 Blunder has rascal guillotined (5)

5 Place trap carelessly and this could be upset (9)

6 Worker gets king a drink (4)

7 Youth to generate transformation (8)

8 Hard-hearted? Girl not so much! (8)

13 He attracts constituents but only with difficulty (2,1,7)

15 God's in charge of working animal (9)

16 Utter nothing in between (8)

17 Superior reduced strike (8)

19 Stick semi-digested food with jelly (6)

20 Model wearing fewer clothes? (6)

23 Travel across German mountain range (5)

24 Jacob's wife finds the meadow hot (4)

Solution see page 250

7

Set by Picaroon

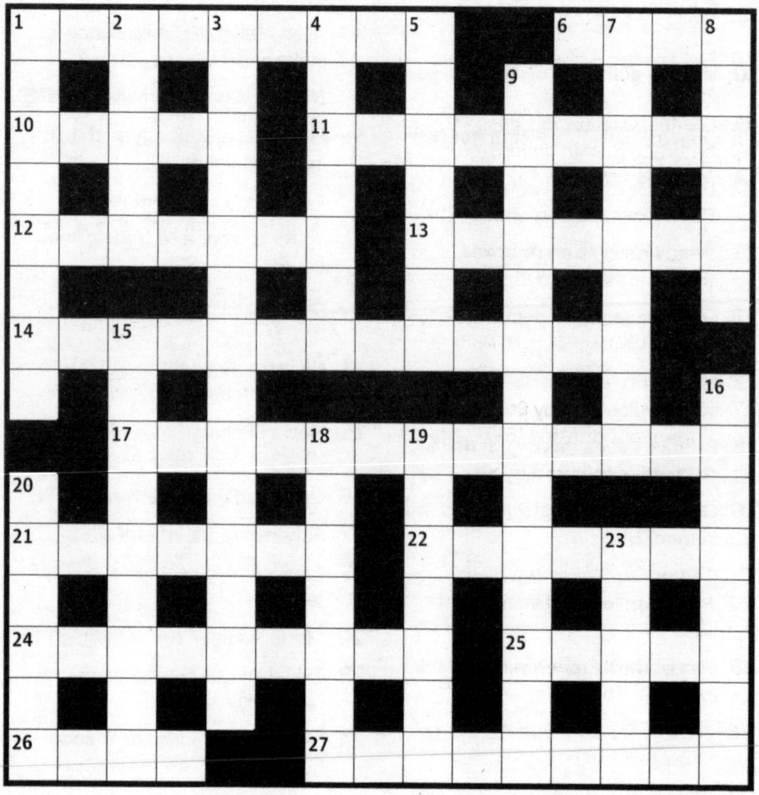

ACROSS

1 Hack off foremost of oenophiles, tucking into supermarket bubbly (4-1-4)

6 Gets on stage, scared to undress (4)

10 Gold colour wheels around Fiat (5)

11 Confused fellow felt desire to embrace men in uniform (9)

12 US writer's feature about rock band making a comeback (7)

13 What I do to keep Angelica or Rosemary sweet (7)

14 In which to strip off layers of apparel, with chests heaving (4,3,6)

17 I'll be welcomed by Stefan Edberg out drinking (6-7)

21 Regulation rejected by nitwit who lives in southern Belgium? (7)

22 A lot of pressure: I'm not sure youngster will accept it (7)

24 Fruit man loaded into blue van (9)

25 Parties with French wine, gallons put away (5)

26 Jackets for keen army about to show pluck (4)

27 Almost out of new porridge, one will surely get the breakfast (5,4)

DOWN

1 What sportsmen try to win, about to miss shots (5-3)

2 Person who's no good for one, flipping bum (5)

3 Comprehensive school had Serbo-Croat Society (6-3-5)

4 What's taken angrily from dodgy dealer (7)

5 Militaristic state, country after power (7)

7 Soldier welcomes a coarse Italian hero (9)

8 Extremely serene and steady (6)

9 Does one do yoga and do they bear the suffering? (9,5)

15 Inferior doctor has name at the bottom of roll (9)

16 Diagnose suffering in such a state (8)

18 It's as touching to be candid (7)

19 Setter up for nude modelling (7)

20 Not going straight like Oliver? (6)

23 A lot of jealousy over one's final words (5)

Solution see page 251

8 Set by Tramp

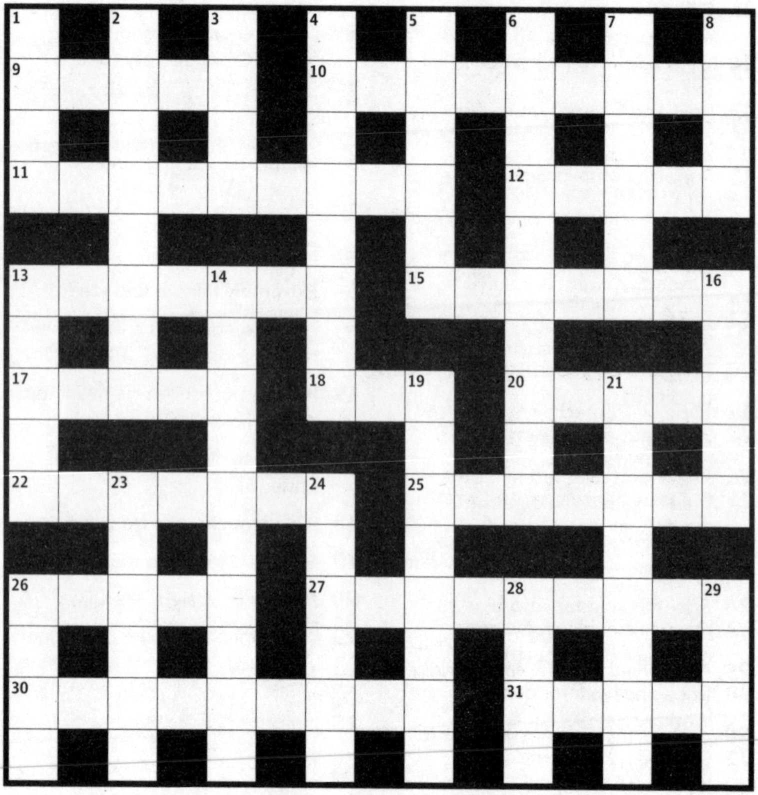

ACROSS

9 Place for Australian Open with no covers: right hot (5)

10 On grass, ace for McEnroe? (9)

11 Salvation Army supply pre-paid envelopes to drop off (9)

12 See 23

13 Husband (Tramp) repeatedly covers meat not on barbecue (7)

15 Rubbish tennis player in America (7)

17 American through to final of slam gets beat (5)

18 Andy Murray's traditional outfit has no length for tackle (3)

20 Cringe to be in debt, going into credit (5)

22 Backs out of space by us: he backs things on wheels (7)

25 Chips in, cooking: goes out with sandwiches (7)

26 Coached British and took drugs (5)

27 Place for tennis elbow: mind needing treatment (9)

30 Does one work for queen? Worker to exploit queen (9)

31 Cold butter at front of picnic hamper (5)

DOWN

1 Geek from small school (4)

2 On which net hangs in Centre Court (8)

3 No more work for retail outlet (4)

4 Star lost set after a chance (8)

5 Summary one takes off copper (6)

6 See man (coach) read out name (10)

7 Good start for game (6)

8 Contract office boss (4)

13 Beat champion in tie (5)

14 Forcibly take mad McEnroe away (10)

16 A queen wearing sister's dresses (5)

19 It's rising? Country ignoring national water level (8)

21 Sense hard tie: pull out (8)

23,12 Bachelor and host drunk with Sue Barker (6,5)

24 Very humid round part of South Africa (6)

26 Love child (4)

28 Left one tie (4)

29 Never taking part in Australian Open (4)

Solution see page 251

Set by Boatman

ACROSS

1 Criminal boss — the first one died violently (6)

4 Gang joined by Italian-American stripper? (6)

9 Call to stop lying in new hoax (4)

10 Helping or turning back detective taken in by this criminal racket (10)

11 Tomorrow, exchange money for Bahamas' foremost fruit (6)

12 Hunters, winging it in battered deerstalkers, dare to go out (8)

13 Part of gun detective loses points to a Scandinavian location (9)

15 Eat into racket with threats at its core (4)

16 Fight roughly, getting head knocked off (4)

17 After a dispute, subdue with sweetener (9)

21 Fixed charge for flycatcher (8)

22 Of late, wrong to demand with menaces (6)

24 Here in Ohio, crime reported twice (returning thanks, Boatman) (10)

25 Sarcasm not unknown as a weapon in the US (4)

26 Detective on racket: "It's fishy" (6)

27 Deal with body of crime writer (6)

DOWN

1 Recite Farewell, My Lovely from memory (2,5)

2 US lawman conceals memory of tragedy? (5)

3 If man performs evil acts, charge him — leaders included (7)

5 Menacing suggestion: loser beaten up with rifle butt (2,4)

6 Prohibition: having three in charge (9)

7 "Pole lifted stolen goods" — that's an informer (7)

8 Examine local yokels — to put through the wringer (4,7,2)

14 26 perhaps the result of acid attack on hotshot in California (9)

16 Criminal libel: "US thugs" (7)

18 Where organised crime penetrated society that rejected drink (7)

19 Tough guy who investigated more lawbreaking (7)

20 Not exactly The Big Sleep, taking DNA in abduction case (6)

23 Gang gets time over botched raid (5)

Solution see page 251

ACROSS

7 King and Serena clash — one's telling tales (7)

8 At front of shop: "51p for each runner" (7)

9 Rock, for example, is overweight (4)

10 Seize the day! Right, I'm off to tour short version in the country (4,5)

12 Feature about a group (5)

13 Elephant eloped with another beast (8)

15 Hybrid engine from Subaru still ends in trouble (4)

16 Criminal fears being more trustworthy (5)

17 Incline discs without rims (4)

18 Filter paper finally covered in coffee, perhaps? (8)

20 British car maker scraps bonnet for body part (5)

21 Conservative's naughty romp — is journalist included? (9)

22 Mockumentary star casts off river vessel (4)

24 Sharp little boy follows conclusion (7)

25 Jack Goulding's desserts (7)

DOWN

1 English bowler won by some top spinning (4)

2 In two short months Yankee takes ecstasy and marijuana (4,4)

3 Fire meat to seal in vitamin (6)

4 European travel accident involves old lift (8)

5 I slap cast over the finale of Oliver Twist (6)

6 Woman's first expensive present (4)

11 Stands for manifestos (9)

12 Reportedly heard by many at Wimbledon? (5)

14 Groom quiet about knight pinching bride's bottom (5)

16 They protect special openings (8)

17 Drink served at party at the top of the Empire State Building? (8)

19 Nut regularly falls, day after day (6)

20 Lots of Chinese food wants starter (6)

21 Block of wood supporting edge of cupboard (4)

23 Welsh boy has fourth beer? (4)

Solution see page 252

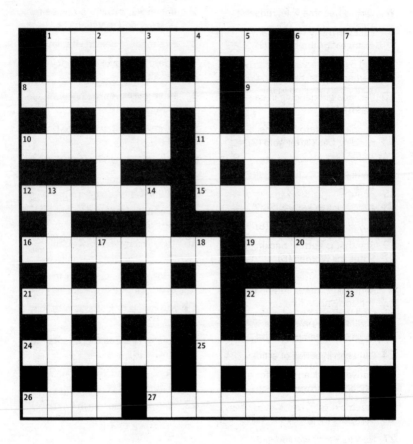

ACROSS

1 Get stricter reporting on match: "Ahead by a big margin" (7,2)

6 Girl, to become wife, runs out (4)

8 East Germany without any changes for the better (8)

9 Girl overwhelmed by rattle — perhaps it makes a loud noise (6)

10 Perhaps girl dancing in cage is harlot? (6)

11 People like Nero in Rome, always heading back after gold (8)

12 Girl and boy married with prayer book (6)

15 Boatman might try this to catch girl: "Want to get excited?" (8)

16 Boy slips out, perhaps (8)

19 Boy that is getting backing for Votes for Women (6)

21 August: one month before April, unusually around end of June (8)

22 As a married woman, her organisation procures an end to injustice in damsel, perhaps (6)

24 Girl seen in series of articles (6)

25 Native American ritual for boy, say, and reformed church (3,5)

26 Foremost of girl's relatives always nurturing (4)

27 New in! Percy worked with another boy to put into code (9)

DOWN

1 The lassie is not even a flirt (5)

2 Ill-informed judgments have visitors losing time around the Home Counties (7)

3 Heartless teenager in meal featuring tropical fish (5)

4 Boy and not boy (7)

5 Party leader built up a fabrication to provide security (3,2,4)

6 Boatman's really odd, being neither animal nor vegetable (7)

7 For cultivation, ordering a New World flower (3,6)

13 One who digs heavy metal in club, either boy or girl, say (4,5)

14 Translated article about principal of using barrels to deliver oil (9)

17 Boy makes move in dance with girl (7)

18 "The young get nutrients from this cola" — Sky broadcast (4,3)

20 Boy, handy without being challenging (7)

22 Girl, to become wife, keeps name at end of ceremony (5)

23 Fastened shoes with raised design (5)

Solution see page 252

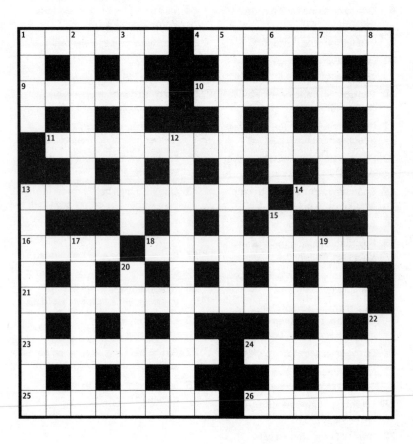

ACROSS

1 Boris's hair? Prime minister cut the ends off (6)

4 Badly dressed seafood stuffed with cut of meat (8)

9 Like a tree? Dog may have (6)

10 Organ stop is sad — piano worse (8)

11 No way will my relatives be crying here? (4,2,4,4)

13 Hold son? (4,6)

14 Ban means nothing to surgeon (4)

16 Dog, or part of it (4)

18 Is that all you can say? (10)

21 Lacking rigid opinions, I am not offended (2,4,8)

23 Corresponding with one of the family (8)

24 Show pleasure about one turn of phrase (6)

25 In one quarter, no respite at first given to our sailors (8)

26 Hold firm in an endlessly boring task (6)

DOWN

1 Train from Bath East (4)

2 A c-competitor is coming (7)

3 Sort of bank on this route into university? (8)

5 Broadcast a serial, more to cheer us up (5,6)

6 Rockers' old rivals grab exercise bikes (6)

7 Orient's collapse is to come (2,5)

8 Like a lump fish? It's OK (5-4)

12 What makes cowards ill? (6,5)

13 Batsman's aggressive strategy found by accident? (3-3-3)

15 His sounds a possible career? (8)

17 At home more healthy to have respirator (7)

19 Agony, using a dreadful hotel (7)

20 Poor chap's attempt to be sick is heard (6)

22 Clothes one changes in the car (4)

Solution see page 252

13 Set by Vlad

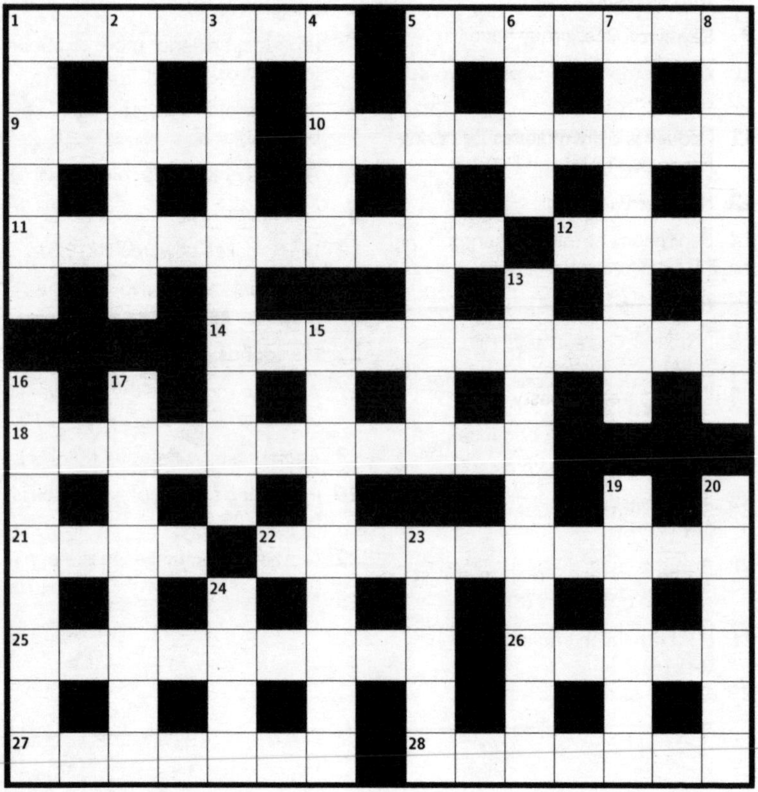

ACROSS

1 In middle of round sheltered by tree (7)

5 Refers to big men, both losing their heads (7)

9 Reviewed, in short, erotica from yesteryear (5)

10 Aid to presentation for Pam (4,5)

11 Thoughts of love dismissed? Fancy one's smitten (10)

12 Number two crosses line — game up! (4)

14,23 "Exciting nights are fiction" (Mrs Vlad?) (11,5)

18 Race, methinks, largely fixed — it won't interest many (5,6)

21 Keep secret Mr Nasty told (4)

22 Soon feel at home because of English on board (6,4)

25 In no way a quack, some might say (9)

26 About to engage with comic hero — it'll provide colour (5)

27 Preference was first to get drunk (7)

28 Course director dismissed sign (3,4)

DOWN

1 Study for a purpose (6)

2 Marvel! Right away is able to have sex (6)

3 Sign I'm struggling with rents in Herefordshire town (10)

4 Winchester's one awfully common pupil gets detention (5)

5 Liberal hit back: "It's unfair!" (1,3,5)

6 Villa centre half welcomes tie (4)

7 Full of energy, play with new guide (8)

8 13 from TV castle — hard (3,5)

13 Go to this place saving time, then do a flit (3,3,4)

15 Decorate country house for the King (9)

16 Dominating male Henry caught unawares (2,3,3)

17 Mike supporting Bill Edmondson and Don? (8)

19 Book a top fighter (6)

20 Yes, vice-admiral's first to go above (6)

23 See 14

24 Possibly saw money being picked up (4)

Solution see page 253

14

Set by Puck

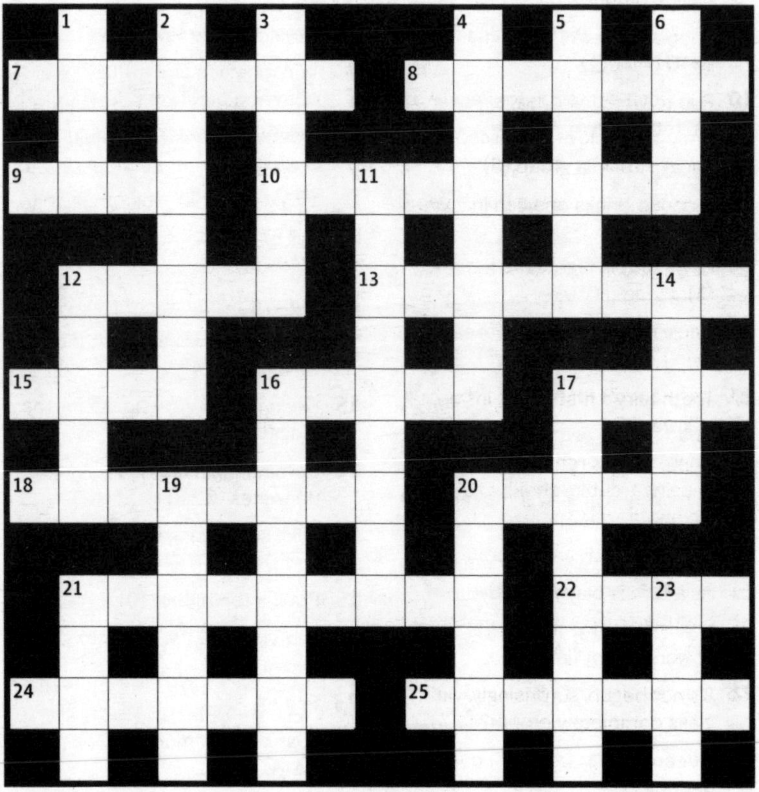

ACROSS

7 Gaunt son in hospital, briefly very sick (5,2)

8 Time on leave: endless misery, having bit one's other half? (4,3)

9 Supports breaks regularly offered by 10 (4)

10 Pub to which Spooner's working girl retired (5,4)

12 Page? He's in a group (5)

13 A comic drinks one can in store (8)

15 Ugly lump in conflict with model (4)

16 Witty remark, providing theme (5)

17 Tooth fairy's first name, inscribed in silver (4)

18 Came across retired people causing trouble, coming to violent blows (8)

20 Spy eating a French sandwich (5)

21 As a turn is played in Haydn and Schubert? (9)

22 Power bills for flats (4)

24 8's not begun, surprisingly, with glass completely empty? (2,5)

25 Queen getting weak, beheaded at once (7)

DOWN

1 Evil originally seen in Jack the Ripper's work? (4)

2 View of the 18 protagonist getting caught, not run out (8)

3 Fool commonly eats guts of fat bird as delicacy (6)

4 Flower seller's first flower show in Covent Garden? (8)

5 In drunken state outside 10, with glass full to the brim? (2,4)

6 Acting on day lost for words (4)

11 Film horrible short adult that's incontinent (9)

12 Gin topless dancer's drunk without coke (5)

14 Small number in 10 upset group of players (5)

16 Bit on the side? Lock phone card up first (8)

17 Guardian secretary in KFC ordered two items less than perfect order, stomach-wise? (4-4)

19 Rod, after a great deal to drink, falls over (6)

20 Quarrel where vehicle gets rammed? (4-2)

21 Book of plays (4)

23 Toy Manx sheep? (4)

Solution see page 253

Set by Picaroon

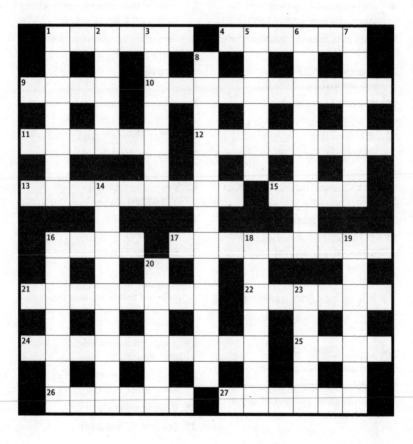

ACROSS

1 PM once ditching head of state in Barnet (6)

4 Retiring soldiers work with country prone to infiltration (6)

9 Drug that doesn't work for man? (4)

10 Medical substitute aces academic assignment (10)

11 Information on length for supporting beam (6)

12,21 What makes daughter a palace attraction? (8,3,5)

13 American rockers make time for artist (9)

15 Coat's wrapped round figure (4)

16 Billionaire's acquired island (4)

17 A feature film's about manual worker (9)

21 See 12

22 Works out riddle, having succeeded finally (6)

24 Doing without six-pack, having drunk 9 etc (10)

25 Rounds with ham, more sandwiches (4)

26 Slightly tight clothing for damsel in order to go around (6)

27 Good God! This is a bit of a pig (6)

DOWN

1 Bully's horrible nature, one admitted? (7)

2 Addle-pated or highly able? (5)

3 Star's sleeveless garment lifted completely (7)

5 Cost of no longer popular piece of music (6)

6 After a few balls, berobed queen's running wild (9)

7 Penny wearing Eve's top? (7)

8 Killer arrested by lawman, getting sudden comedown (6,7)

14 Missing king to get dubbed ignorant (9)

16 People wearing religious clothing (7)

18 High tea during hard period for concubine (7)

19 Fifty Shades-type behaviour an unwelcome sight in the bedroom (7)

20 Lascivious, heartless church bigwig (6)

23 Signal recalling marines (5)

Solution see page 253

16

Set by Tramp

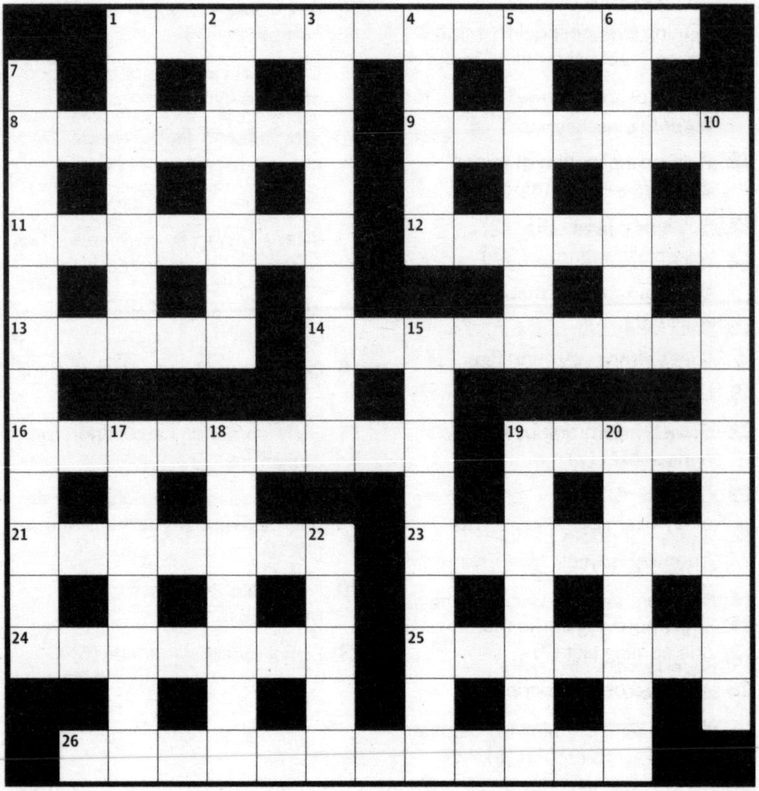

ACROSS

1 Difficulty going on after Ascot tip in racing (12)

8 Economic recovery over? Drink round noon (7)

9 Turning over channel to catch series — set off for film (7)

11 In that place (South America) for May? (7)

12 Help on inclination of talent contracted by newspapers (3,4)

13 Splits payments (5)

14 Ruling men replace head of banking with director (9)

16 Swaps one-time lover and makes a connection (9)

19 Ladies' man, Tramp, in jumper (5)

21 Something stirring by cheat's right pocket (7)

23 Old half of Victoria line starts to delay users getting tube (7)

24 Catching Boycott's return, nearly got it (7)

25 One improving in the morning, one coming last (7)

26 Annoyed one preparing for TV (5-7)

DOWN

1 Part of toilet cold on one's rear (7)

2 Those fixing cars — Reliant's part turned up (7)

3 Follows name and number over a line (4,5)

4 Missing royal standards round five English flags (5)

5 Screwing books up — possible complaint of typist working (7)

6 Feeling that makes some cry? Pain regularly piercing (7)

7 Early star with banker set out recklessly (6,6)

10 See 19

15 Developing Aldi: Tesco put out (9)

17 Jimmy Carr, with offshore banking, primarily fiddled (7)

18 Building issue when housing Victorians? (7)

19,10 Let's take most of Harrison Ford's fantastic film (7,2,3,4,3)

20 Rabbit's mother put to sleep (7)

22 Stiff with or without female on top (5)

Solution see page 254

ACROSS

1 What gambler may do, missing unknown signs (8)

5 Assurance from a doctor about pallor in odd places (6)

9 Is it driver James or MP Jeremy reported persecution? (5-4)

11 Religious adversary, not half grotesque (5)

12 Hedonistic ways of husband, following dainty pair of girls (8,4)

15 Warning what a misandrist wants? (4)

16 African in evening wear and I attack Scot (10)

18 Unfriendly bird's way to kick horse, say (4,6)

19 Poet's lost face, having wagered money (4)

21 Hoping to get a small ratio using integers (12)

24 Big star back to bowl a slow delivery (5)

25 Deplores what top managers are paid? (9)

26 Loves entertaining composer, not one to dramatise (6)

27 Fellow feeling inhibited accepts to lightly touch setter's back (8)

DOWN

1 Assistant with navy, one of many on board (4)

2 Key element of air for singer (4)

3 Stick bill on present (6)

4 Muttered furiously, poked by weighty girl with a stick (4,9)

6 Paul left distraught, making some scoff (8)

7 Invalid, incorrect legal document one cuts (10)

8 Shot or pass defender's stifled (10)

10 Annoyingly, criminal stole my investing money abroad (13)

13 Bird eats hot dog, possibly uncertain (5-3-2)

14 Fiddle with glass covering hotel — you can see through it (10)

17 Dawn light caused a shock (8)

20 Ruler and predecessor of Sun King, one with power (6)

22 Don't delete this shot's frame on film (4)

23 See tablets pharmacy's packaging (4)

Solution see page 254

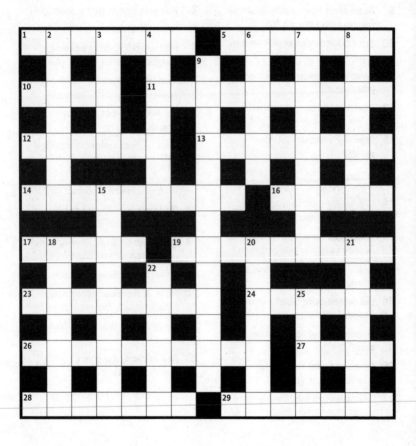

ACROSS

1 Welsh 24 has criminal brothers, except Henry (7)

5 At the end, Number 10 mislead Britain with spirit (3,4)

10 $50 + O + 5 + ¼ = O$? (4)

11 Daughter's into grooming over time, keeping up appearances (10)

12 Mark's drumbeat (6)

13 Old car, since exterior lost in jam (8)

14 F or M, like Marilyn Monroe? (3,6)

16 Inner Hebrides partner (5)

17 Dared to tremble with fear (5)

19 In ancient times, say, raised flower (9)

23 Football team in nasty ground winning first game (1,1,6)

24 Steal about 1p's worth (6)

26 Published paper retires girl over nothing? Inconceivable! (10)

27 Torture's not even legitimate (4)

28 Normally left Australia and America going west (2,5)

29 Embrace internet 16? (7)

DOWN

2 Smelly old dog ran to ex, shaking every tail? (7)

3 Competition rising in cost? Never! (5)

4 Prat stumbles over low bar (7)

6 Awkward size OK for sumo wrestlers? (6)

7 Shakespearean doctor's credo: bury sick (4-5)

8 Produced positives and negatives when treated as a celebrity, going topless? (7)

9 Burning petrol joins up to produce power (3,10)

15 Spring day weather returns with southern Europeans (9)

18 Maybe in the future Arsenal condemns Sun after Gary's hacked (3,4)

20 Office workers found to be tipsy, swooning over good man (7)

21 Abbot's put on posh new shirt to remove ties (7)

22 Decipher pointless meaning of puzzle (6)

25 Old-fashioned mister exchanged letters underground (5)

Solution see page 254

Set by Vulcan

ACROSS

7 Caretaker's start-of-year rise (7)

8 Top copper? (7)

9 Put a sock in it (4)

10 Revile dad horribly, being a reckless type (9)

12 Aerated bath in Don's place (5)

13 Heartless superstar gets speed (8)

15 Curse as front breaks off explosive (4)

16 Spell of delight (5)

17 Pawnbroker's wife? (4)

18 Destruction is wonderful (8)

20 Announced spaces for loading coarse cloth (5)

21 Takes responsibility for rubbish users hold (9)

22 States waistcoat is small, in check (4)

24 Where fashion advice appears popular (2,5)

25 Seeing poorly, get glasses finally for book (7)

DOWN

1 Party? Try to have one (4)

2 Hacking, will fear this security measure? (8)

3 The last to get such a spoon (6)

4 In grandfather's case, a regular swinger (8)

5 In the cold, shake and shatter (6)

6 Carry away proceeds of robbery (4)

11 Shape of playing field a mess (9)

12 Energy of son, 11 ... (5)

14 ... nervous energy, after 10s (5)

16 Kid almost a yob? Relax (5,3)

17 No light opinion formed by the critical (1,3,4)

19 No spinners coming up? Absolutely right (4,2)

20 Hamper such a hopeless case (6)

21 Go down its plughole? (4)

23 Lampoon Saint Christopher (4)

Solution see page 255

Set by Shed

ACROSS

1 Socialist supporter securing a British isle (6)

4 Good person keeps longing for container (6)

9 Landlady's army (4)

10 Mineral cup — one dropped by academic before end of ceremony (10)

11 Look hard, taking in 5, and go hungry (6)

12 "Drug arrest" in dog Latin? (8)

13 Litigant's unsophisticated argument (9)

15 Plant nothing in drink (4)

16 Reliable sort of music (4)

17 Mark with sorrow, keeping Catholic back from crop protector (9)

21 Church painter, perhaps, or reformer (8)

22 Have words with motorist of sorts, catching cold (6)

24 Stupid stories about journalist's headmaster (10)

25,2 Capital of 15, mostly, getting turban adjusted (4,5)

26 Things discharged from cortege, startlingly (6)

27 Sound of instrument gives sign (6)

DOWN

1 Concerning anterior part of flat iron dropping one off (7)

2 See 25

3 Old emmet's nice mess absorbed (7)

5 A headless whale keeping a number of secrets (6)

6 Chair duly arranged to be driven by liquid (9)

7 Part of roof covering spaces that may be stretched (7)

8 Hardening Muslim leader receiving 100 — one hundred — a hundred divided by one (13)

14 Cop for fit that's beyond remedy (9)

16 Find new home for ambassador held up by wake (7)

18 Tough composer endlessly set in stone (7)

19 Supreme general (7)

20 Strip joints given time (6)

23 Drink, in the old days, uplifted cartoonist (5)

Solution see page 255

ACROSS

5 Get under someone's skin, might it? (6)

6 Painter related to darkest shade, as he used to say? (6)

9 Test buoyancy ultimately in fish (3,3)

10 Attack top and bottom (8)

11 See 18

12 Erect using poles etc, obvious long parts (5,1,4)

13 Where a bridge is bent (2,3,6)

18,11 Go on sponsored walk primarily, middle of week taken off (6,4,4)

21 See 22

22,21 Applies oneself, like a gorilla? (8,4)

23 One is oddly patchy (6)

24 Ticklish rear of lieutenant aroused (6)

25 Ursine, might you say? Just about (6)

DOWN

1 Organ composition in fruit (8)

2 Cunning clue for "dump illegally" (3-3)

3,7 Getting frisky, Catherine dated bit of a looker after divorce? (8,6)

4 Ice has to remain in order (6)

5,20 Near catastrophe, question getting involved in hideous US-Korean war (6,6)

7 See 3

8 Matt, perhaps, in 5 20 (5,6)

14 Little time in sport for speeding (8)

15 Damaged by run, boy runs indeed? (8)

16 Poetry like this half–cut poet served up (6)

17 Wet under thatched roof of the rural gentry? (6)

19 Who could be in court loading a revolver? (6)

20 See 5

Solution see page 255

22 Set by Crucible

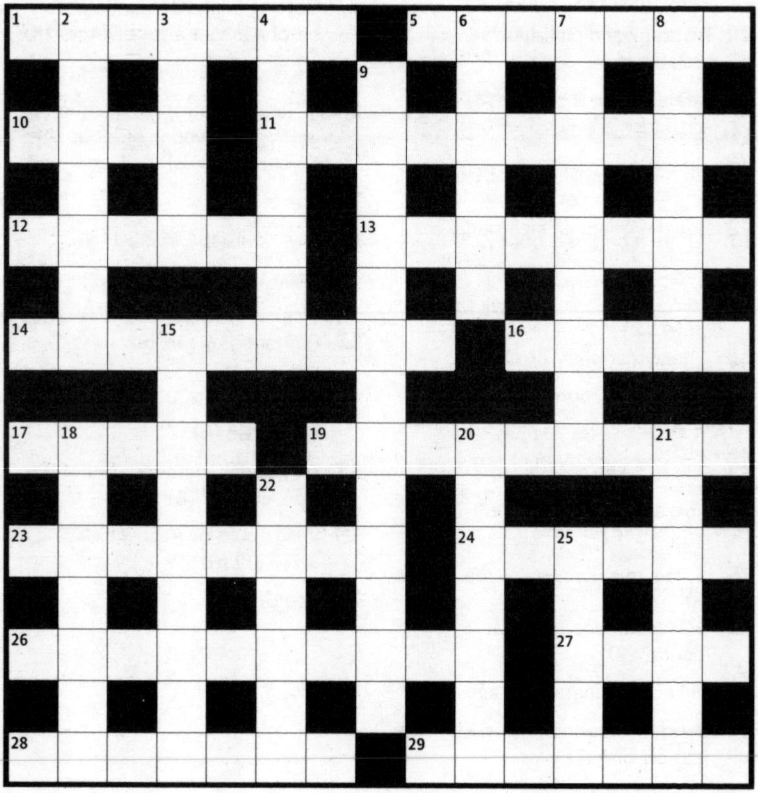

ACROSS

1 Book was wrong about current state of some trees (7)

5 Information is inspiring French art creation (7)

10 It's black and pink, lacking resistance (4)

11 Dash back before crossing forbidden Silk Road for one (5,5)

12 Zinc or rocky mineral in crystal form (6)

13 British–American sign said: "Coach Line" (3,5)

14 Building material makes smoother sound (9)

16 Quarryman's key picked up (5)

17 Practicable round safety device (2,3)

19 A paper nobody backs maintains run for some time (9)

23 Bismuth has to turn red, perhaps piebald (8)

24 Tell bishop, not priest (6)

26 Don't read enough to be a locum? (10)

27 Unknown mineral long ago (4)

28 Send for treatment here, after he falls off bike (7)

29 Contestant receives surgery for disorder (7)

DOWN

2 Bizarre objects, each full of toxic compound (7)

3 Corporal remains Roman Catholic priest at heart (5)

4 Former Tory leader in court is dead and gone (7)

6 Stevenson's written about still (4,2)

7 In Brussels, book into sprawling development (9)

8 Gatecrash lewd independent theatre first (7)

9 Period yielding 10 addled brain? Of course! (13)

15 Find nightclub dead (9)

18 Dodgy dealer rings excellent pottery (7)

20 Peer that follows just after the start (5,2)

21 Rock formation exposed by harvest (7)

22 Ancient 3 fellow East German left (6)

25 Liberal philosopher's bed (5)

Solution see page 256

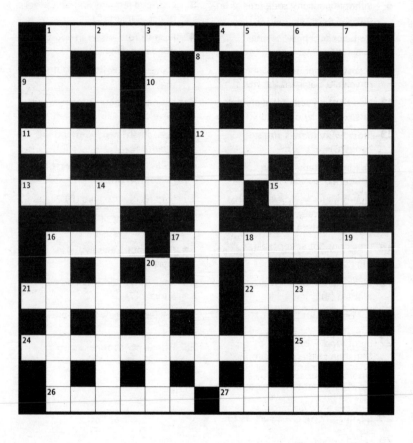

ACROSS

1 Using sophisticated kit, there's a snag about energy (2-4)

4 Suitable publicity precedes short musical entertainment (6)

9 Homework pages — school subject to be absorbed (4)

10 Makes audacious gesture in front of vehicle, being insane (10)

11 Heart shown with initial change of sex — tricky operation (6)

12 Most floury food is situated to be eaten (8)

13 Like an academic discourteous about computers etc? See about that (9)

15 Lady, not totally square, wanting bit of adventure (4)

16 President not acceptable to top people, strangling a party (4)

17 A second attempt to describe unusual moon in science (9)

21 Home with red exterior? Blow me! (8)

22 Bit of food — bit eaten by Christian soldiers repeatedly (6)

24 Liberal bod upset by this sexist toy? (6,4)

25 Grasses grow upwards, as you might say (4)

26 Good person with halo maybe in train (6)

27 Order complied with, note having been sent back (6)

DOWN

1 Dog in item of luggage, hot rather than cold (7)

2 Editor-in-chief drank excessively (5)

3 Firm Madame leading heritage organisation evokes criticism? (7)

5 Caught by cameras, callous rogue (6)

6 Row's beginning to interrupt quiet book? Damnation! (9)

7 Vehicle is a heap — pity that can't take me (7)

8 Soldiers of African country imprisoned in country? That's becoming standard (13)

14 Writer interrupting the German reporter (9)

16 Songs terribly sad after dance (7)

18 About to settle or break up? (7)

19 Fool is left drowned in drink (7)

20 Trainee as part of a performing act in the auditorium (6)

23 Cut up? Hard to show gaiety (5)

Solution see page 256

ACROSS

1 French writer reversing endless nonsense on theology (6)

4 Bricks exist to stop possible splashback? (6)

9 See 15

10 Polish sign features in books (10)

11 Local love in action, how alluring you are! (6)

12 Current times in pieces one's read (4,4)

13 Character upright, as client awfully stiff (9)

15,9 Looking troubled, like Mississippi, might you say? (4-4)

16 Denounce grand sporting feat (4)

17 Rig out sweetheart with very old dresses, getting upset (9)

21 Person setting light rocks around a very heavy rock (8)

22 A boring cocktail? (6)

24 After tramp, father separated to find second mother, say? (4-6)

25,3 Nature observes possible sign-off? (4,7)

26 Old player finding minimum of peace in dove ... (6)

27,23 ... as dog circling tree caught by artist (6,5)

DOWN

1 Witnessed female drinking last of Chardonnay — how much? (3,4)

2 See 20

3 See 25

5 Reject is punching floor (6)

6 Cradling baby initially, voice calmer (9)

7 Huge female goddess inhabiting tiny island, briefly (3-4)

8 Bedtime exercise making a difference on submissive types (8,5)

14 Dog has head on armchair in comfortable place like that (5,4)

16 Poisoned cups clean originally, I doubt (7)

18 Sports event, on gun this always starts (7)

19 Constant lack of leadership in one winger tackling another (7)

20,2 Taken off air twice, opted for clandestine transmitter (6,5)

23 See 27

Solution see page 256

ACROSS

8 King enters affair with army corps backing — he has weapons (8)

9 Novel serving of mashed potato? (5)

10 Racing driver family's rise (4)

11 Dry sort of northern £1 note across the sea (3-7)

12 Energy produce by sun in equivalent type of oil (6)

14 Hand back old man left in Gap (8)

16 Church doorkeeper moved to Syria (7)

18 Shrink one spoils (7)

21 High Tory capers will do (6-2)

23 When to be rejected by wind god (6)

24 Neglect your garden plants? Not on the surface (10)

26 Suffering light that's pronounced (4)

27 Hastings has, on the outside, abandoned incense (5)

28 A people fit and willing (8)

DOWN

1 Footwear riddle (opening's moved to heel) (8)

2,26 Bird sound, piano and song — it's murder! (4,4)

3 Grand farmhouse fruit, good for nothing (6)

4 Go in pursuit of pleasure without currency, old man! (7)

5 Nation of Trump senior, a major power no more (4)

6 Play area feature? Not exactly (10)

7 Drugs that are incorporated into shoes (6)

13 Tai chi term for development work on figures (10)

15 Reverse dancing? Precisely (3)

17 Name a god ending in Y (3)

19 Thigh or rib lead housing far from attractive (8)

20 Bringer of tidings needs support — Mother Nature, primarily (7)

22 Produce charged particles and celebrate topless (6)

23 Way a good sort nurses Rowan, perhaps (6)

25 Wife, decline to carry on! (4)

26 See 2

Solution see page 257

Set by Philistine

ACROSS

9 Hector is by definition adorable (9)

10,5,18 Tree surgeon's plant is about right for me (5,6,8)

11 In retreat to meet up: majority of one, missing a member (7)

12 Got together in hospital with a composer (7)

13,25 Exploit dispute minister rejected in agreement (8)

14 Shabby at interrupting dog instructions (4,2,4)

15 More delectable than a salmon terrine is egg roll for starters (7)

17 Actual consumer suffers with a twist in the tail (3,4)

19 Planning a set dinner to finish badly (3,2,5)

22 Formerly one in a hundred? On the contrary (4)

23 Object to experimental mice being present locally (7)

24 What to wear in case? (7)

26 Preserved member of an ancient civilisation (5)

27 It's King Lear BBC can blame for losing odd characters treatment (5,4)

DOWN

1 He just appears gentle around climax: he made it up (5,2,3,5)

2 Eliot, Eliot & Eliot (8)

3 Gone sinister (4)

4 See you when you arrive, but not first off (2,6)

5 See 10

6 Had an impact on camp (8)

7 Shops here are holding scoundrel (6)

8 Still confused about a copy of the Iliad? (3,3,5,2,2)

16 Half in the dark and troubled in my disgrace (8)

17 Hears endless adverts? Not with these! (8)

18 See 10

20 Conclude being educated not at fault (6)

21 Thrill from sexy act with her unclothed (6)

25 See 13

Solution see page 257

Set by Chifonie

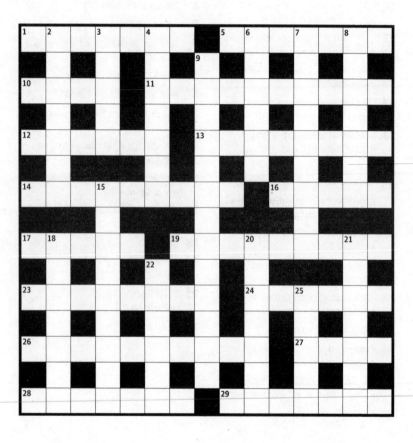

ACROSS

1 Base person's cloth hat (7)

5 Shelter, formerly in a state (7)

10 Business is settled (4)

11 Means of transport, showing first-class pedigree (5,5)

12 Doctor is curt and unrefined (6)

13 Autocratic cops tied suspect (8)

14 The Parisian wears suit when cold (9)

16 Jam in a piece of cake (5)

17 Almost finished writing for share certificates (5)

19 Ally improbably felled in front of ship (9)

23 Expert discovered to have great insight (8)

24 Corrosion wore away pivot (6)

26 Folly of Romeo interrupting disrespectful behaviour (10)

27 Marks time with silver pole (4)

28 Pupil's in time to get support for school subject (7)

29 Working out, Nat aims for staying power (7)

DOWN

2 Ambitious banker has great taste (7)

3 Seduce casual worker over time (5)

4 Soldier in pub is reasoned (7)

6 Bungling bosses continuously fill the mind (6)

7 Soldier without energy is not spiritual (9)

8 A riot is developing (7)

9 Supercilious prisoner's going down (13)

15 Strengthen and control troops (9)

18 Animal carries artist? That's sweet! (7)

20 Iron workers in right tizzy (7)

21 Figure it's a month since opening of nightclub (7)

22 Split up left-wing union (6)

25 Transport grand icon (5)

Solution see page 257

Set by Picaroon

ACROSS

8 Reserve hotel with flower in cool place (8)

9 Ambassador, found with smut, is calm (6)

10 Wader's good sense on westward track (6)

11 Slate masons remove (8)

12 Dash in road, back to the start (4)

13 Landlord's stewed tripe scoffed by approving soldiers (10)

15 Vain fellow with sense to wear jacket of organdie (2,2,3)

16 Sulphur and more acid in dish (7)

18 Worn after study, lawyers must don article (10)

19 Russian front east of Iceland's capital (4)

20 Problem around heroin, with opportunity to shoot up (8)

22 Bent lawman gets round the law (6)

23 Wife gets joint that's beef (6)

24 Pretender wants pastry, having uncovered buffet (8)

DOWN

1 Perspective from train, even if stopping regularly (6,2,7)

2 Supply inn with hogsheads, now disclosing plans (7,4,4)

3 Judge and posh tax criminal sat next to one another (10)

4 Potent smell's caught that's representative of pupils (4,3)

5 In the current circumstances, fool takes one in (2,2)

6 English run grim economy badly: things'll get ugly! (2,4,2,4,3)

7 2, perhaps, means 6 (3,6,3,3)

14 Scientist's lady's cross, oppressed by dull routine (10)

17 Like some leaves having two buds? (7)

21 Outstanding poet's encouragement to unite (4)

Solution see page 258

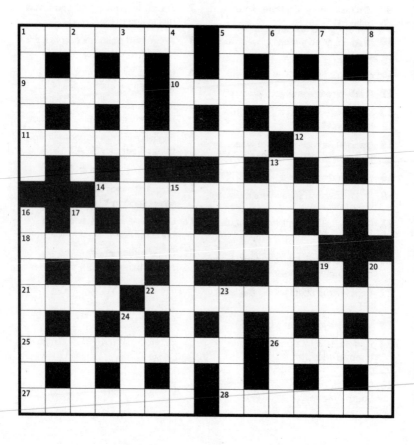

ACROSS

1 Bait cricketer (7)

5 Casual attempt to secure image (3,4)

9 Get out good fashionable clothes (3,2)

10 Spooner up for distortion by design (2,7)

11 Pretty boy playing with Arsenal (10)

12 Wet grass (4)

14 Good health looking problematic then? (3,2,4,3)

18 European enquiry given testament in sharp, English wit (7,5)

21 Machiavellian shackling Catholic, I see! (4)

22 Train to capital crossing river, its effect disorienting (7,3)

25 Setter reversed a state that's flow (9)

26,17 Drug dealer, one often over the limit? (5,8)

27,19 Make up accent, funny case of boring joke (3,4,4,2)

28 Rock garden ends, we hear, in South American capital (7)

DOWN

1 Field ball (6)

2 Active as an actor? (2,4)

3 Decent result of spring-cleaning? (3,2,5)

4 Drink draught up, guzzling juice (5)

5 Underground worker, Dickens character ending on burdensome early shifts (4–5)

6 Initials of tiresome egotist revealing my name (4)

7 Trotters cut, evidently bleeding, cleaned (8)

8 Judge accepts bound to be more happening? (8)

13 Operative in USSR, possibly peripherally as foreign agent (7,3)

15 A pinhead introduced to pub grub as a toddler? (2,7)

16 Just winning, prepare for a fight (6,2)

17 See 26

19 See 27

20 Some turkey heads and old goose wings filling dish (6)

23 Charged I note, first sent off (5)

24 A shade flatter (4)

Solution see page 258

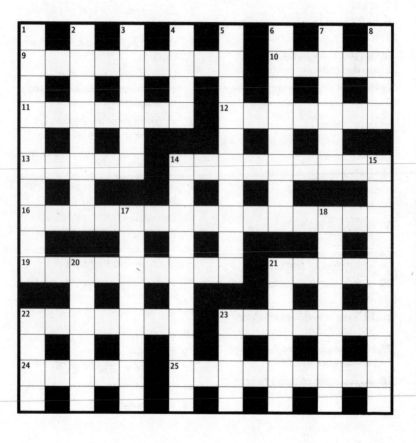

ACROSS

9 Cut, but not polished, when suggested? (5-4)

10 English invading prosperous foreign state (5)

11 10 caught during escape don't count (7)

12 Keels over, having striven in conflict (7)

13 Remarkably old theologian disheartened laity (5)

14 Brave comic ultimately loses interest in script (9)

16 Recondite manoeuvres protecting two hospital departments in secure housing (9,6)

19 What's put out for famous moggy, perhaps on Yorks coast? (3,6)

21 Bond's partner formerly occupying Students' Union (5)

22 Person striving to keep motorways in better condition (7)

23 Husband's lacking in flair — a cure-all's offered (7)

24 Manufacturer of cars, many with posh interior (5)

25 Tsar's necessary after turn of century and easily dealt with (2,7)

DOWN

1 Case supporting idle property owner (10)

2 White rebel is obliged to guards (8)

3 It's said capacious hanky's needed, if you're like this (6)

4 Had a life before wife turned up (4)

5 Confused detective hampered by gut reaction (10)

6 Cleric appearing on donkey in church causes deep division (8)

7 I stray off course in South American mountains (6)

8 So close, having swapped ends (4)

14 After fancy exercises, band's sobbing quietly (10)

15 Confirmed nickname for Edward, the ocean sailor? (4-6)

17 Complex seminars not quite hitting the mark (4,4)

18 Charge imposed on a variety of basic commercial vehicles (8)

20 Particular Democrat isn't first to yield (6)

21 Sergeant, say, getting up one day full of himself? (3-3)

22 Son's leaving even now to work in field (4)

23 Course of action at entering pub? (4)

Solution see page 258

31 Set by Paul

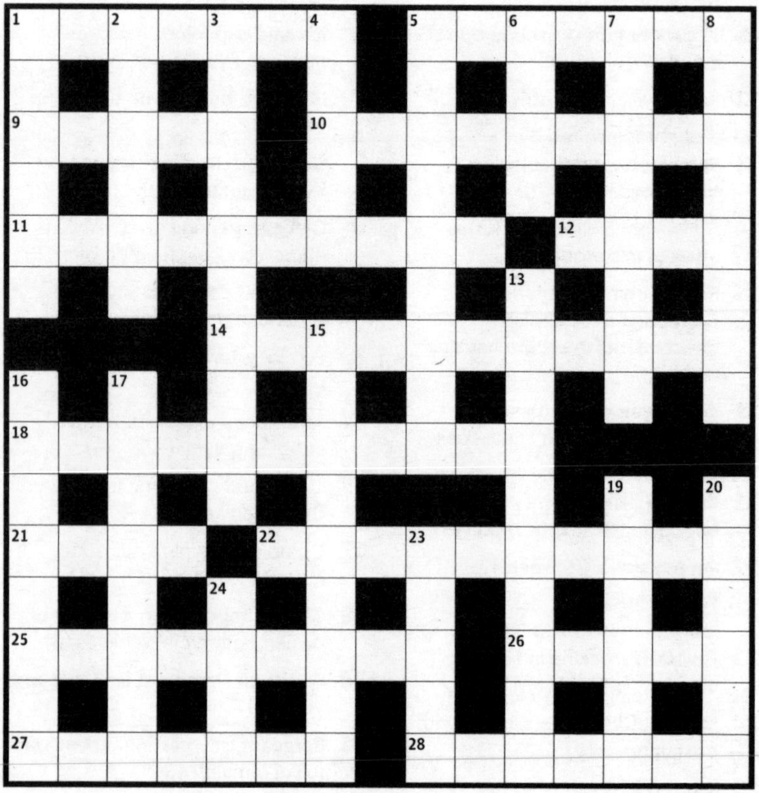

ACROSS

1 Admirer pulling sausage skin from dish of game? (7)

5 Into loveless jive/salsa dancing, am I potty? (7)

9 A success for Lloyd Webber, somewhat inevitably (5)

10 See 25

11 Daughter inspired by the influence of granny, perhaps, after heading for shower to get cleaner (4,6)

12 Avian that's smoked (4)

14 Gloucestershire opener in desperate chase dropping catches — players get lessons here (5,6)

18 Fine lifesaver having stepped down, one in the majority (8,3)

21 Head shaved in bed; that's proved painful! (4)

22 Man offering personal advice, lunacy gone mad! (5,5)

25,10 Feeling initially around letter bag, need letters for children's favourite game? (9,9)

26 Sweet thing hard to forget in ancient Chinese text (5)

27 Little jerk inspiring one to beat giant (7)

28 No explosive energy for runner (7)

DOWN

1 See 4

2 Welcome in outskirts of Ontario, an American statesman (6)

3 Best thing to bury a spy, so desperate to feign death (4,6)

4,1 Joint declaration of nation, great effort (5,6)

5 Fickle type appeared to welcome leadership of Hitler and Trotsky (9)

6 Womaniser's tool (4)

7 Point put in to ham about right for butcher's device (4,4)

8 Single weapon briefly in contact with a Roman emperor (8)

13 Cruise too flipping grand for PC travel (10)

15 In eating badly, chips primarily causing immune response (9)

16 Weak figure entering testament in support of the devil (8)

17 Intellectually threaten to push city's outsiders around (5,3)

19 Fighting, it arises during a party (6)

20 Beginning to brag, bird hunter (6)

23 Stretcher on after awful injury, demolition all ends up (5)

24 New painting lifted hero (4)

Solution see page 259

32 Set by Paul

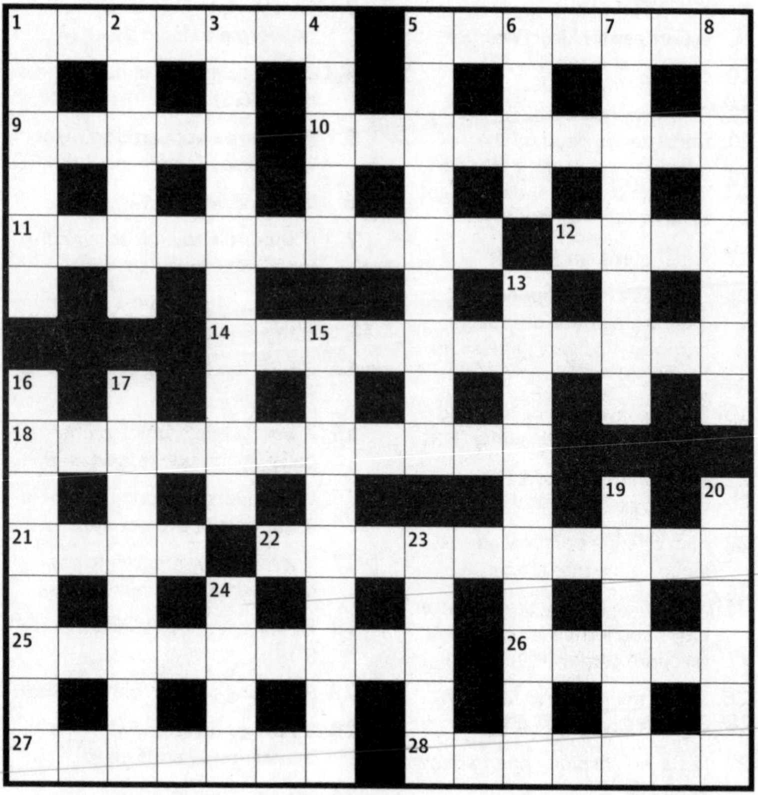

ACROSS

1 Pudding, not starter, interrupting fish dish (7)

5 See 26

9 Forever turning old and dirty, every second lying back (5)

10 On with it! (9)

11 English author the Guardian's translated is back on the box (10)

12 Fishwife who survived? (4)

14 In basic parts of music, end improvised around heavy metal for maestri (11)

18 Deals with cities built to be stretched? (11)

21 Bound to need patience, ultimately — a virtue? (4)

22 Dressing prime minister, one is an oddball (10)

25 Short garment beginning to rise in sketch by a couple of artists (2-2,5)

26,5 Old group ending in tub can't get c-clean? (5,7)

27 Gain in knots with set distance travelled (7)

28 Outside broadcast on golf tournament (4,3)

DOWN

1 Club welcoming hot talent (6)

2 State that is dividing America, pants? (6)

3 With rigging of ballot admitted, suits go to pieces (4,2,4)

4 Five into nine, the rational number (5)

5 Greek dramatist breaks to pocket first of cash, after bribe (9)

6 Alcoholic drink preferable, not teetotal (4)

7 A philanthropist controlling computers proves perturbing (8)

8 Dangerous Goth losing heart in the clutches of wicked Irish king (4-4)

13 Venial story about Pasquale, perhaps? (10)

15 Blinking Titanic sunk, no good (9)

16 Delicate creature, speaking clock needs to rest voice? (8)

17 Some fortification in fleece and horns, for example? (8)

19 Capital cheers outstanding nation (6)

20 Cock and hen? (6)

23 Trump gone, party! (5)

24 Drink a can, almost (4)

Solution see page 259

33

Set by Vulcan

ACROSS

1 Fail in court recess (6)

5 To sleep, say, on bed, one may lie on one's back (8)

9 Friendly hint (8)

10 Protecting goalie's job (6)

11 Only interact corruptly? No way (9,3)

13 Traffic lights always red? Not possible (2,2)

14 Previously, but never again? (4,4)

17 Invoice of a sort for working poor farm (3,5)

18 Announce I own a place for spiritual retreats (4)

20 A British division raised by the Romans (8,4)

23 Wife, the most beautiful girl in America? (6)

24 A lordly brew? (4,4)

25 Fashionable people get new mattress (5,3)

26 Trendy humorist has success (4,2)

DOWN

2 Using a little plunger, take a breather (4)

3 Lose concentration, so stop watching TV (6,3)

4 Each in sequence for drink dispenser (3,3)

5 Not concede one has to store spare bed linen (4,1,5,5)

6 Does one deserve a lighter sentence? (8)

7 Knowing, for example, about two volumes (5)

8 Party getting together, not rebelling (10)

12 Reporting for work (10)

15 A misfortune in constricted part of car (4,5)

16 Part of the Union in a right state (8)

19 Strict, requiring name on pointer (6)

21 Pipe up (5)

22 Some advise minister in the House (4)

Solution see page 259

34

Set by Boatman

ACROSS

7 Carp and turkey with cream (3–4)

8 Collects fish food from wild roof gardens (7)

9 Fish quiver with head cut off (4)

10 A shocking thing: having an even keel, rescuer stepped in (9)

12 Wanting some monkfish or turbot (5)

13 Boatman is at once overturned (8)

15 See 17

16 In the US, a sinker in leading edges of drag or net under trawler (5)

17,15 Naughty fish plot to steal things (8)

18 Boatman accepted into crew: no problem for a beginner (8)

20 What you need to make out with this fish! (5)

21 On foot, they're bound to steal from depots for Spooner (9)

22 Polish off fish food right away? (4)

24 Is caught in wood? That's fishy (7)

25 "It's not fair!", shouted fish out loud (3,4)

DOWN

1 Capital of Libya, leaving by motorway instead (4)

2 "Took back control of nothing": expression of disdain, bearing much tedium (5,3)

3 Perhaps grave speech: get rid of euro, in part (6)

4 Stickler for skill in middle of aiming trap for fish (8)

5 Source of comfort for heel contained by fish (6)

6 Encourage caviar maker: just take heart (4)

11 Odd fish set to one side (9)

12 Spear sunfish (5)

14 Salmon got by special method on line at top of tide (5)

16 Dispose of fish food (8)

17 Defence of cod, skate, flounder (8)

19 Brill, catfish gutted with gusto, finally chilled (6)

20 Cold tuna's prepared for one in Italy (6)

21 It's a bit fishy, but anglers buy it (4)

23 Principal material for sinker (4)

Solution see page 260

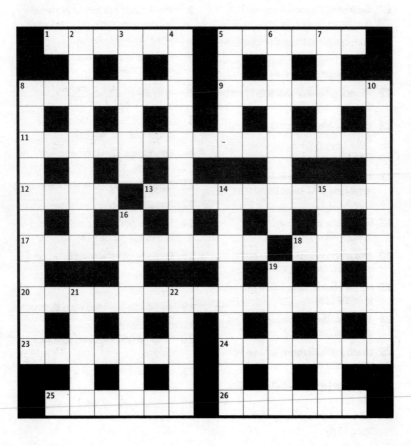

ACROSS

1 Relaxes muscles for drug that is injected (6)

5 Walked closely behind man, European went first (6)

8 Rubbish inside most of chicken drumsticks to go on these? (7)

9 Run a bath to get over upset (7)

11 Playing at Euros: result in sudden-death shoot-out? (7,8)

12 Beginning to get it with date (4)

13 Time to appear earlier in big dress: Oscar for actress (5,5)

17 Short fellow against guys being attached to this troublemaker (10)

18 In blue, fanatical football supporter (4)

20 Telegraph work? It involved being on wire (9,6)

23 Former nurses work to provide food for children (7)

24 Tips to collect working for peanuts (7)

25 Learner that is after a pass, then one can drive on farm (6)

26 Sugar to look sexy when cycling (6)

DOWN

2 Attractive woman needing a lot of money to strip (9)

3 Awful to recall Hamlet at end of plot (6)

4 Web developer enters PIN that's incorrect (9)

5 Creature in river? (5)

6 They stop racket abuse — Sharapova temper finally blows (8)

7 Flipping tense, smoke and belch (5)

8 Mahler: that's refined music (6,5)

10 Travelling easier on coach going around city (6,5)

14 One might go off chest dating site put at top (9)

15 These might secure lock at back: not keys to house (4,5)

16 Quiet party game (8)

19 Writer of piece returned grant (6)

21 It could run down wall? Wee covering floor having missed opening (5)

22 Section of wardrobe seems large (5)

Solution see page 260

ACROSS

5 All over the place, miss catching ball that's gone up (6)

6 Fast pace cut, time cut back (6)

9 Asians in a queue, say, captivated by bit of a looker (6)

10 Old couple in the family way rejected, might these take some heat off? (8)

11 Fairy caught by vampire, pixie in retreat (4)

12 Flatulence offensive, put a knot in it! (7,3)

13 Kindling after log can catch fire (11)

18 Covering article inoffensive? (10)

21,5down Pants one regards where bloomers on display (4,6)

22 Wrong part of house noted well enough? (8)

23 Caught, famous Smith and Wesson finally turned over (6)

24 Missile sees helmsman in river shortly reversing (6)

25 Inspector Lynley's first scrap (6)

DOWN

1 Buzzer in tiny temple arguably for announcement? (8)

2 Capital, sharp tool used in action? (6)

3 Drunken reveller, driver stopped by officer originally (8)

4 Star key, look (6)

5 See 21

7 Common talk a steamy thing on Love Island (6)

8 Look at artist's uncovered bed, shocked (11)

14 Farm animal tucking into provender served in a flash? (8)

15 Furthest behind, I started to crack up (8)

16 Prompt perceptible to the audience? (6)

17 A heaving of water on top (2,4)

19 Encourage operator to doff cap (4,2)

20 Free horseboxes for animal involved in a blood sport (3,3)

Solution see page 260

37

Set by Nutmeg

ACROSS

1 Where habitual drinker goes, suffering a loss, too? (4,3,7)

8 Plant that comes with strings attached (5)

9 Better rail transport brought back, impossible earlier (8)

11 Little piggy sheltering at home with old ram (3,4)

12 Soldier in country area, Italian student centre (7)

13 More cunning Times puzzle ultimately rejected (5)

15 Colour of prince's blood? (5,4)

17 Chart for walker's aid, mountains and plains primarily added (6,3)

20 Antique from ancient city, one with firm casing (5)

21 Distressed tenor given a wigging (7)

23 Thieves pinching 50 speakers (7)

25 Steep terrace unoccupied behind mooring area (8)

26 Book — almost completely useless ... (5)

27 ... novel by Sitwell and an ex-PM (7,7)

DOWN

1 Spineless type upset by puppy in middle of speech (12)

2 Hospital injection needed in wrenched spine (5)

3 Food from buffet car? This won't normally cover it (5,4)

4 CO cuts route devised for green excursion (7)

5 Engineer, say, up to late examination (7)

6 Grouse, perhaps beginning to rant with more spirit (5)

7 Unofficial Irish king holding a gun up (9)

10 How a username is arranged for storekeeper? (12)

14 Distinguish between lines embraced by far right group — almost (4,5)

16 Phone contact habitual drinker often makes? (5,4)

18 Macho guards fighting Trojans et al (7)

19 Fuss over British cook's seasoning (7)

22 Counterfeit offering — any odd bits must go (5)

24 Bowler not right to bend it? (5)

Solution see page 261

38

Set by Maskarade

One solution embraces 10 others, which lack further definition.

ACROSS

1 Amaze old fellow swallowing bit of gristle (7)

5 Flower disturbs Lettish characters (7)

10 Some of the Baggies coming back (4)

11 Language from rogue upset eccentric (10)

12 Golden couple's young domestic worker (2,4)

13 Stand surety against posh church roof repairs (5,3)

14 Unfortunately, unable to include Tooting's follower (9)

16 Initial investigation into family line (5)

17 Ain't professional (5)

19 Over half a dozen links of forty years ago (9)

23 Theme of Jews out West admitting identity (8)

24 I am nicked — no way — and charged (6)

26 Well-bred people, quiet and not from the county (10)

27 Rich uniform covers (4)

28 Dance and workout teens arranged (3-4)

29 Turned off tragedy (7)

DOWN

2 Officer's platform (7)

3 Midnight in Georgia (5)

4 Clapton hugs politician and setter — a quack (7)

6 Call to account at university after reporting dining area (4,2)

7 Not at home and sadly is shut outside (5,4)

8 49 is enough, but ... (7)

9 Salesman getting small delight in plant (10,3)

15 They weren't Liberals it turns out, dropping left (9)

18 Female has lived at moonshine outlet (7)

20 Father raised girl (7)

21 Former City off-road vehicle to perform (7)

22 Head worried about getting stick (6)

25 Block artist (5)

Solution see page 261

39

Set by Picaroon

ACROSS

4 Drops bags for one to recover (6)

6 Hack lies with part in column (8)

9 Repressed writer to behave like a randy animal (4-2)

10 Where financiers are still doolally (8)

11 One launching projectiles knocked over player in the slips (11)

15 Wrong marks doubled in current exam (7)

17 Failure to recall men deployed in the East (7)

18 Allied with Italian, twice scoffed about leader here (11)

22 Sort of cream pudding, one from Raymond Blanc (8)

23 Dispensing with clothing, avow gods root for cult (6)

24 Climber's endless hunger to be among celebs (8)

25 Uncovered part of New York, a holy city (6)

DOWN

1 £51 in cash (6)

2 Make gloomy record on the period we live in (10)

3 Raves where ecstasy's dropped by an underground warrior (8)

4 Old artefact broken by boozer in China, say (8)

5 Game to have a couple of drinks? That's surprising (3,5)

7 Marshal competitors needing to strip off (4)

8 Is he a pain in the neck? (4)

12 Enjoy capturing knight in Paris, who is to surrender (10)

13 Setter makes unfair remarks about Irishman, perhaps (8)

14 Leader no longer touring round country (8)

16 Frame opening demand of horrid letter (4,4)

19 Does one run away? I'm not sure about run (6)

20 Device that sucks up a drink (4)

21 Over sixteen letters (4)

Solution see page 261

40

Set by Qaos

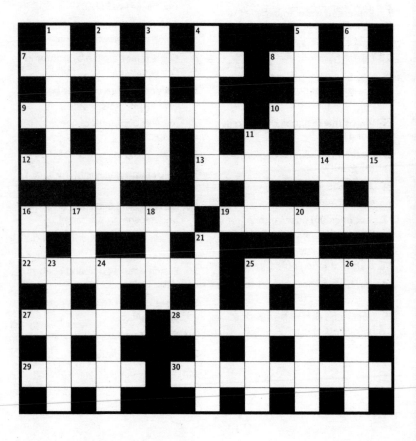

ACROSS

7 Officer with prisoner not changing (9)

8 Driver annoyed Miss Right (5)

9 Queen caught pole dancing at Royal Academy (9)

10 Judge rejected patter as "gas" (5)

12 Husband's at home, tucked in bed — it's late (6)

13 Irate Dane resigned, partly over song (8)

16 At first, you can die horribly from this? (7)

19 Drink with singer and guide (7)

22,25 Priestly symbol worn by 1 down? (8,6)

27 Greek character regularly rushed treat (5)

28 Crying out to put elite in jail? Not half! (9)

29 Royal unit involved with charge? (5)

30 Really not joking (9)

DOWN

1 Dog runs away from miner (6)

2 European playing tennis, holds ball to win ace (8)

3 Firm covers up unknown American threat (6)

4 Shopkeeper first out? Look inside (7)

5 Fellow drank up endless port and married woman (6)

6 A liberal in the field (6)

11 Charge without rupee? (4)

14 Tree house, like on top (3)

15 Trim facial hair to get attention (3)

16 Trump, perhaps, 2 clubs over 1 (1,1,1)

17 Drink made from malted barley's common ingredients? (3)

18 5OO11OO1OOO deciphered by Private Eye (4)

20 Explorer's post: "Lost new vehicle" (8)

21 In English court, in Leeds, mostly (7)

23 More flamboyant Formula One driver, it is said (6)

24 Sorry, a criminal makes up prayers (6)

25 Review covers up journalist's reputation (6)

26 Chronicles of Narnia's leader Aslan are fantastic (6)

Solution see page 262

41

Set by Nutmeg

Solution see Page 236

ACROSS

1 Bubble that irritates second-rate movie star? (7)

5 Deal with vexed solicitor on the phone (4,3)

9 Suspicious sailor retraced Cuban's steps (5)

10 Man from our sphere transformed? (9)

11 Children paired for walking races feigned distress (9,5)

13 7 academics and students cross (4)

14 Cruelty always preceding sex, in skivvy's case (8)

17 Useful headgear, they say, for a horse race (8)

18 Prophet taking his son back is looking older (4)

21 When nothing went right — nothing! — he'd often say so, angrily (3,2,5,4)

23 String of cars transported Democrat round Ohio, principally (9)

24 Considering the odds, trust your coach (5)

25 Clouds over rescue vessel impeding retreats (7)

26 Virgin placed in lower recessed tomb, historically (7)

DOWN

1 Flyer's attempt to cross river (4)

2 Going under gangster's arm, it'll raise the temperature (9,6)

3 Shock as pioneering PM ditches Queen (6)

4 Those left without uniform to hang out (6)

5 Trader moving comparatively freely round island (8)

6 Artist, prig at heart, secures collector's items (8)

7 Android perhaps showing how things are done in theatre? (9,6)

8 Red sky is beginning to turn with brisk pace to the north (10)

12 Space needed in Slough after Mothers' Union expanded (10)

15 One particular service a strain for Anglicans (3,5)

16 What travels within France's country tracks? (8)

19 Like to strip off when retiring or having a snooze (6)

20 Journalist re-stocked it, ordering pens (6)

22 Good clear network (4)

Solution see page 262

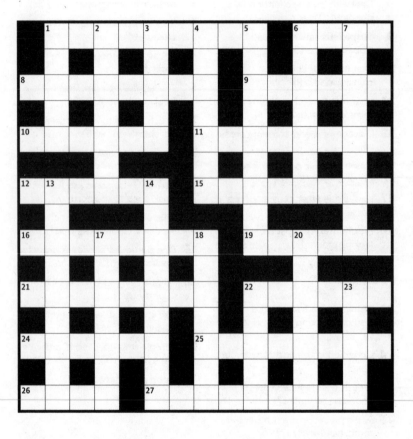

ACROSS

1 Dance clubs serially introducing followers of Paddy Clarke? (3-3-3)

6 Poor clue's back to front (4)

8 Refined tincture into which is dipped a second pen (2-6)

9 It could go off with a bang in Hollywood this evening (6)

10 Chapel in Dumfriesshire bearing name of Roman city (6)

11 Out of true love, lady finally managed hugs (4-4)

12 "Pasta rings": line in new Alien (6)

15 Regret turning over like one reaching North Pole, say (8)

16 Allowed bill to add up, so this wine sent back (8)

19 The way to work round Emerald Isle sheep (6)

21 Rabbit initially trapped by African, then catching a dim-witted friend of his (4,4)

22 Loveless woman of some allure to set about Valentine's rival (6)

24 Strong liquor street bar had in short supply (6)

25,14 A prominent hole — the suspect ... (8,2,3,4)

26,27 ... how should we respond? Not at all (4,7,2)

DOWN

1 Something Indian women wear during public holidays (5)

2 Someone for young athletes to look up to? Mo's leaving town (7)

3 Water, perhaps, let me think it's deadly boring (5)

4 Butler cracks enigmatic clue — so not hopeless! (7)

5 Net is cast in a suspicious part of a defensive system (9)

6 Rebellious set cuffing suspect seen to get nervous (5,2)

7 Commonly used as frankfurter dips? (2,3,4)

13 Tutee not excited about nucleus of charged or, possibly, uncharged particle (9)

14 See 25

17 Great disappointment for ice cream lover? Topping embellishment (7)

18 Queen's name included in list for Swampy? (7)

20 Chap last in Tour: "I don't want any more cycling!" (7)

22 Personal training rep (very important person) killing Three Coins in a Fountain (5)

23 I'd find out which items are odd, perhaps even (2,3)

Solution see page 262

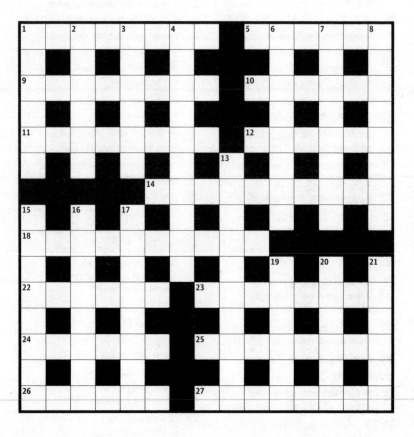

ACROSS

1 Case of vehicle speeding (8)

5 Maps all bombs shelled with nonchalance (6)

9 En passant, victim turns left just before the end (8)

10 Slogan is mostly a device for catching people (6)

11 Lad's fancy in 26 turns to 15 20 (5,3)

12 Board emergency meeting starts by tree outside (6)

14 Back between the sheets and topless, such very decadent behaviour (10)

18 Rushes round container for Harvey and Co (10)

22 Understood Saudi princes essentially playing (6)

23 Fuel hurting around half of common people (8)

24 Using combined power to undress shy bride (6)

25 Ship first to feature in opera composition (8)

26 Season well (6)

27 Dine out having little money? It's not proper (8)

DOWN

1 Bone from rooster — half a dozen, say (6)

2 Squire turns 27 (6)

3 Top to bottom in past form of 26 minor accidents (6)

4,19 Unintended consequences of local alert (10,6)

6 Where drugs are fast to suppress hurt (8)

7 Shocked to have revealed sexuality in newspaper? On the contrary (8)

8 Bruise for servant trapped in bottle banks (5,3)

13 Fabric helping injury (10)

15,20 Romantic ideas should be found in loft? Shove off! (8,2,4)

16 24 excluding part of goal (8)

17 Papers over dream separation (8)

19 See 4

20 See 15

21 Since strike, displayed brotherly love? (6)

Solution see page 263

ACROSS

8,24down Train's hour late, extremely annoying — the usual reason? (8,4)

9 It's briefly about a particular case, gripped by disease (6)

10 God in fallen idol making a comeback (4)

11 Stars wonderful, though the first eclipsed in constellation (10)

12,3 Man bandaging cuts, his wares often thorny? (6,6)

14 See 22 down

15 Initially raking in money, half of this ancient city (7)

17 Teacher regularly catching head turning, concentrate (7)

20 Old actress eating only cream cakes? (8)

22 Cool in deep space (3,3)

23 Scenario unfolding on busy route, somewhere in the northwest Pacific (10)

24 Sound wheel part (4)

25 Wife hasn't provided wicked little pest (6)

26 Most desperate youth retrospectively securing passes (8)

DOWN

1 Reportedly far from excited with topless greeting in house of ill repute (8)

2 School where every Tory of note starts (4)

3 See 12

4 Fire a colleague from Belfast? (7)

5 See 19

6 Tracksuit perhaps fits uphill runner (10)

7 Nerves of steel? I think not! (2,4)

13 Social gathering in competition with divers at sea (5,5)

16 Complex relationship ending in disaster, one in imbroglio (8)

18 Unaware your challenge can't be completed (8)

19,5 Delusional activity, drink evil stuff in whisky with violin players (7,8)

21 Painting is about to come up (6)

22,14 1970s' fashion, flaming dull clothes exciting people (6,8)

24 See 8

Solution see page 263

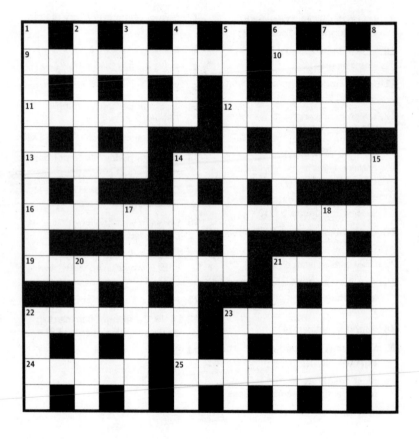

ACROSS

9 Industry for high flyers rapidly embracing lust (9)

10 Call to reduce phobias (as justice ought to be) on Tyneside (5)

11 Hypnotised with spots of light instead of softly snoring (7)

12 Without a word of thanks, left in London? (7)

13 In bonds, hopes (5)

14 Fortitude beside explosive device found at highest level on vessel (6,3)

16 They include envy, with idle sadness in some versions (5,6,4)

19 Dog sled is worked in shifts (9)

21 Eastern root of many outsiders ornamenting life in capitals (5)

22 He employs cowboys with spurs, no nonsense, wiser at last (7)

23 Dish sent back, Boatman saying: "No meat" (7)

24 22 down's confused, where victory lies in virtue (5)

25 Always strong and stable but inside loveless, therefore concerning (9)

DOWN

1 Destroyed by devils and a radicalised ... (10)

2 ... Soviet leader, restoring Ivan the Terrible, last letters of literati lost (8)

3 Small change to charity creating sacred music (6)

4 Slothful doctor gets home help (4)

5 Jesus' words of comfort for the poor in spirit etc: "Go and renegotiate dues!" (10)

6 Heroically, ecstatically proletarian: no hothead, no alternative (8)

7 Looking up to quote work of lyrical quality (6)

8 Soviet leader on former Axis: "It's hot" (4)

14 Scene of overindulgence and wicked bare greed by name? (4,6)

15 They guide the coach's team after taking number one with pride (10)

17 One freshly converted to make war, say (8)

18 One unfortunate formerly embraced, then cut off (8)

20 Some tabloid on showing temperance (6)

21 Note: wrath is an illusion (6)

22 Losing some faith finally in prudence, causing split (4)

23 Raised Soviet leader to become first (4)

Solution see page 263

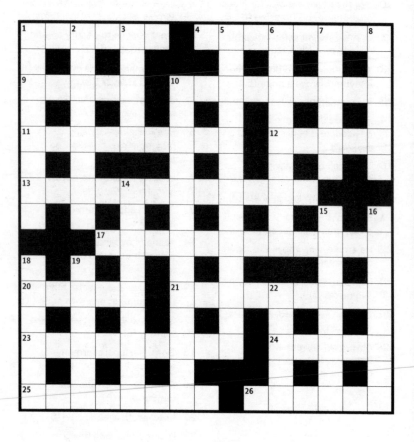

ACROSS

1 Band to undress, ultimate in disgrace (6)

4 Big story about the same big health problem (8)

9 A king brought by seaman to a port (5)

10 Bishop needing to phone wife maybe to prove a point (5,4)

11 Conversation sure to be rambling after party (9)

12 Material provided by poet rejected (5)

13 Fie, ban diesel! Unlikely not to be done away with (12)

17 One worker in East going after fish oil (12)

20 Bird left on far side of river (5)

21 Huge seat falling apart outside old lodge (9)

23 Possible clue to 'erod being a sinner (9)

24 What's worn by everyone going round is plain (5)

25 Struggled, being weak at first, then was first after break (8)

26 Given map instructions, drove off (6)

DOWN

1 Mediterranean vessel traversing small lake is poetic (8)

2 Where transport cafe is, notices one that's journeyed around (8)

3 Philosopher with old books having mountain to climb (5)

5 Quiet merriment is organised around 1 May? (5,8)

6 Ailing, I'd start to take new drug (9)

7 Indigenous people rebel endlessly under Communist dictator (6)

8 Sharp Conservative has something to gain advantage (6)

10 Bird from cage, loose, struggling under farm building (8,5)

14 Hot glow of anger in experience with BA? (9)

15 One's featuring in play with no hint of eloquence being required? (8)

16 See this place with car (8)

18 Show deference? Gosh, what a childish creature! (3-3)

19 A Barchester clergyman not on the level (6)

22 Expression of surprise from place lacking redemption and love (5)

Solution see page 264

ACROSS

1 The virtuous aren't found in police force (6)

4 Pack, card player works out, lacking spades (6)

9 Arsenal may display these tight turns (4)

10 Train in a ground after game in a fantastic country (10)

11 Country Britain governed that is overthrown (6)

12 New trio with Man United's legendary menace (8)

13 Notice reporter half-cut before his boss retired (9)

15 Former backs and the like (2,2)

16 Lofted ball in, after header from Chelsea (4)

17 Team — this one's left in small pieces? (9)

21 Ruler knocked back a drink with a poor player (8)

22 Ruddy track by female pop star (6)

24 Interpretative psychologist's opening up Electra complex (10)

25 Unrestrained woman, one who's finished losing heart (4)

26 Check on Saturday's clothing arrangement (6)

27 Solution's to keep City back, the French learn here (6)

DOWN

1 Kane, perhaps on the left, is encouraged (7)

2 Playmaker with affliction in hip (5)

3 Row about blunder, one foxes may avoid? (7)

5 Looking annoyed, wanting power trip (6)

6 Drink abroad and get out lots of drink for game (5-2-2)

7 Flyer nearly cheeks fool (7)

8 Learner's cracking debut fit for top clubs (7,6)

14 The powerful old girl working with cash (9)

16 County towns content to leave drinks (7)

18 Frankly, nothing stops Communist guerrillas with China (7)

19 Men score, cutting through Harlequins' sides, or Wasps (7)

20 One hoarding shows enchanting fellow clothing Greek character (6)

23 English and Scots off target, mostly low score (5)

Solution see page 264

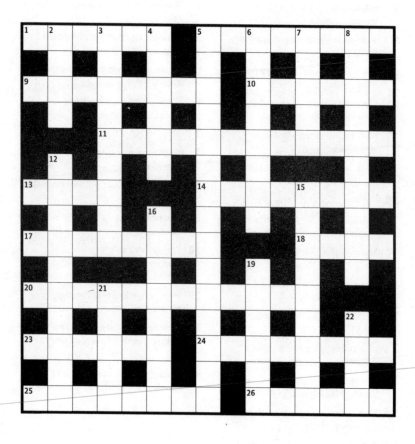

ACROSS

1 Land in Siberia, part of journey being discussed (6)

5 Supporter covering grass for sporting occasion (4,4)

9 Announcement: target has been hit? (8)

10 Hunter put game on stick (6)

11 In which babbling voices rant on? (12)

13 See 23

14 Round of leaflets ending in porch and I almost exploded! (8)

17 Colour to match in gaol (3,5)

18 A figure turns — on this? (4)

20 Knock back and forth (12)

23,13 Scrabble has no guide, no further explanation required (6,4)

24 Lock up the little devil, having rejected classroom show of dissent? (8)

25 Possessions for forward delivery, ultimately (8)

26 Summary, like one this short, ends (6)

DOWN

2 Thunderstorm's beginning, cling to hood (4)

3 Officer's faithful colleague decorated in unlimited expression of remorse (6,3)

4 Range that's 20 in film (6)

5 Defensive attitude that may once have got Tiger Woods out of trouble? (6,9)

6 One doubts a jerk will keep number up (8)

7 Brief stop (5)

8 In fitful pain, wine not finished: I'm surprised! One's always at the bar! (10)

12 Partner of footballer always tackling scorer, one has a job (4,6)

15 Remarkable bird circling peak in Tibet (9)

16 Chaser possibly? I'm not sure one's a hunter (8)

19 Thick sauce and pieces of meat, but no starter served up (6)

21 Strike head of teddy bear (5)

22 Battle in Belgium on Sunday (4)

Solution see page 264

Set by Brendan

ACROSS

9 Diversion — something necessary to get round European soldiers (9)

10 Religious establishment backed vote for protecting bishops (5)

11 Refers to tourist attractions, repeatedly mentioning these locations (5)

12 For start of book, two things a knight has? (5,4)

13 Female not just a provider of entertainment (7)

14 Like some old people here, having reduced fishing around area (7)

17 Final stanza that may be read in broken voice (5)

19 Cast lacking confidence in company (3)

20 Head off old car, producing road rage, for example (5)

21 Portray female author as progressively involved (5,2)

22 Diamonds I'd turned into money, like a rotter (7)

24 Page about fictional hero holding one cold and negative attitude (9)

26 Sense of achievement from hunting animals collectively (5)

28 Demolish east wing of building in a sorry state (5)

29 A short sentence added to American volume without changing any characters (9)

DOWN

1 Crews in race circuit site missing leading article (4)

2 Writer with 27 endlessly able to produce 9 (6)

3 Body covering USA revised one set of beliefs (10)

4 Right part of book — right for father of 6 2, for one (6)

5 Sculptures or other form of art, say, divided by working group (8)

6,8 Romantic heroine, Juliet, with a new energy, Romeo coming into view (4,4)

7 Scraping racket in a game (8)

8 See 6

13 Stop and return, if led astray (5)

15 Musical performance originally arranged round old piano (5,5)

16 PM once linked with partner in 19th-century novel (5)

18 The writer is caught by very upset assistant in compromising position (3,5)

19 Displaying either component of a novel by a lady (8)

22 Author in part of Greece penning article (6)

23 Stupid people do it after change of heart, interrupting lives (6)

24 Explorer in rescue vessel put under pressure (4)

25 For instance, game briefly written up in press (4)

27 Eponymous heroine, such as Madame Bovary (4)

Solution see page 265

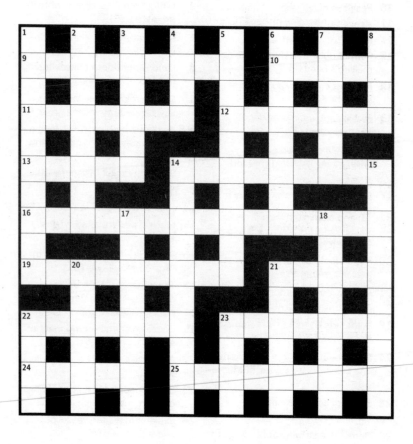

ACROSS

9 All of us sniff a new career (5,4)

10 I love tackling journal's final stage of development (5)

11 Agent of retribution, English, lying in state (7)

12 Former duck trap that is snaring mallard's head (7)

13 Educated girl eating a yogurt dish (5)

14 American ready to separate opposing sides in port (9)

16 Smiley's group jams here in central London? (9,6)

19 Carpeted stable dam wrecked (9)

21 Tin and aluminium locks here (5)

22 Note silence among ladies in bygone times (4,3)

23 Journos, gathering in loose ends, raise them in anger (7)

24 Centre Point's fine old state (5)

25 Song by East End barman is going places fast (3,6)

DOWN

1 Articles about wearing suit in camp (10)

2 Rule for each individual framed by one parent (8)

3 Puzzle's meaning can be decoded without a name (6)

4 Landowner doesn't finish hideout (4)

5 Decide moves after Woman's Own's first brave feat (6,4)

6 Latin repetition not working for bookworms (8)

7 Saw one in Glasgow filling sink (6)

8 Innocent, maybe: a thousand and eleven fled Pompeii (4)

14 Extra maths problem starts to annoy lazybones (10)

15 Not how Ko-Ko operates, lacking spirit (10)

17 Clear fingerprint impressed into actual tablet (8)

18 College on lookout to host large assembly (8)

20 State capital needs a good deal to secure province (6)

21 Clubs and diamonds run out for consul (6)

22 Port given permission to entertain foreign leader (4)

23 Ambassador and bishop's address in 20 (4)

Solution see page 265

51 Set by Vulcan

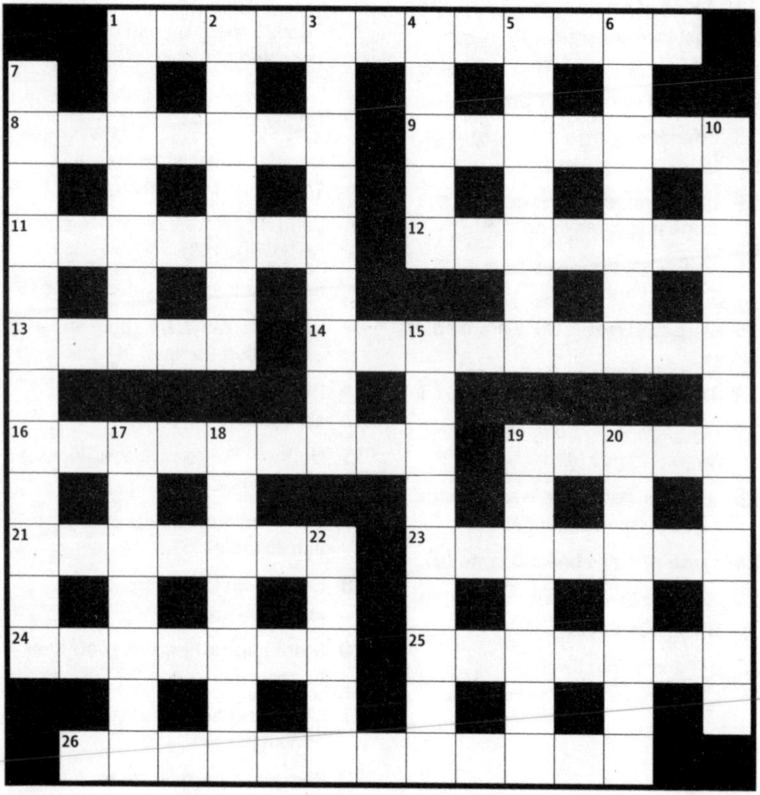

ACROSS

1 Allies report false plot warning (7,5)

8 Scowl from the French in place of healing (7)

9 Most perfect short day in Rome, too (7)

11 Items of data about popular drugs (7)

12 Attitude it's vain to display (7)

13 Turn round with part of foot (5)

14 Cooked best fare, introducing old English favourite (5,4)

16 Immediately suggesting wrong home? (5,4)

19 Animal's sexually ambivalent offspring (5)

21 A daughter chosen to be taken in (7)

23 Somewhat lacking, prune quality is just not the same (7)

24 Recession in a seaside town? (3,4)

25 They go down for a sleep (7)

26 Is it shelved in Swansea? (5,7)

DOWN

1 Edible sort of dog (7)

2 Historic legislation for the police (3,4)

3 A back-breaking weight (4,5)

4 Government holds British currency (5)

5 Look fat, so was unsuccessful (4,3)

6 Lender I tricked, one not to be crossed (3,4)

7 Riots in school, which Marx expected (5,7)

10 One may only have two ties left (12)

15 Cancelling order for troops (2,3,4)

17 The last word in virtue: and extra (7)

18 Bird pecked small tasty morsels (7)

19 Group live on geese, carved up (3,4)

20 More fresh crockery I brought in (7)

22 Fear of snaking adder (5)

Solution see page 265

52 Set by Paul

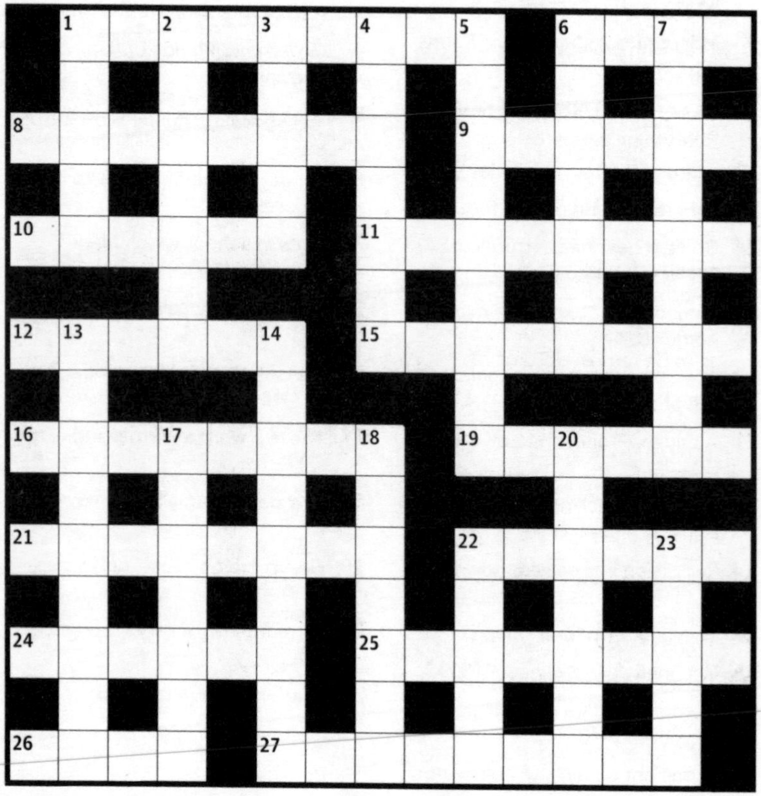

ACROSS

1 A setter held back by someone flirting? A corker, perhaps (9)

6 Day-old wrinkly, age-old character (4)

8 Pray with private for new recruit (8)

9 Muncher of grass munching everything green (6)

10 Day piercing scream almost turned sour (6)

11 Private chamber I reserved to host first of ladies in extravagant fashion (8)

12 Cunning plan — stain at the front is to be removed from shirt (6)

15 Catch outstanding European leader's ultimate revolutionary song (8)

16 One promising to keep mum permanently in gin, drunk by the sound of it? (8)

19 Hill bearing small fruit (6)

21 Soldier in art museum, name Frank (3-2-3)

22 Partner joining principal in company with a generous corporation (6)

24 Ruminant occupying hollow tree (6)

25 Redhead after drunken hack in bar, utterly unyielding (4,4)

26 See 17

27 Sharp instrument happens to nip hand (9)

DOWN

1 See 17

2 Foul word of prayer masked by babble (7)

3 See 17

4 Silk, rather oddly, used for old gowns (7)

5 Grass around fielder picked up (9)

6 See 23

7 See 22

13 Motor race that's cultivated (9)

14 Imagine this crossword starts out as cryptic (9)

17,3,1down,26,20 To demonstrate one's sincerity, eat bread? (3,4,5,5,4,5,2)

18 Paddy beat Republican shortly (7)

20 See 17

22,7 Dawn's sound party at which to sketch spaniels, might you say? (4-1-6-3)

23,6 I, Russian leader, ostensibly tipsy? (5,7)

Solution see page 266

Set by Arachne

ACROSS

9 Get ready, while attracting lots of viewers (5,4)

10 Pilgrimage of posh bloke ends in Andhra Pradesh (5)

11 Pretend one's cool, entering declining years (7)

12 Helping discontented barista around coffee counter (7)

13 Time to abandon cabs for Central line (4)

14 Quite attractive guards finally stop all disruptive conduct (10)

15 Short, slight Arab surrounded by water (7)

17 Put up with some alterations to machines (7)

19 Raving angrily? It's cause of hoarseness (10)

22 Women going into loft backwards to make deliveries (4)

23 Airily attacked Trump's revolutionary deeds on regular basis (7)

24 Communist cobblers in extremely tremulous state (7)

26 Old fellows always lacking manners? Rubbish! (5)

27 Development of gallstone gutted Victoria, for one (9)

DOWN

1 Over 100 Lilliputians sadly accepting love is mirage? (7,8)

2 Stellar couples sign book in advance (8)

3 Hairy humanoid oddly ignoring my meat pie (4)

4 Exit half-cut Finn with scarlet jumper upside down (4,4)

5 Mum returns quietly after month in Split (6)

6 Leader of Greece pricking Europe's uneasy conscience (8)

7 Summons male to move sinuously (6)

8 Awfully shy friend stopping Bob vacillating (6-9)

16 Refuse to be buried (8)

17 Nervous sibling consumes pot, mostly, and heroin (8)

18 A magistrate disrobed after firstly cursing, out of hearing (8)

20 Thin umpire in bit of sunshine (6)

21 Violet's neighbour doing somersaults round island (6)

25 Using speech of Sadiq Khan, say, to oust PM (4)

Solution see page 266

ACROSS

9 Slowly movin' to conceal swindle, a part of Asia (9)

10 Old quarter, newer design (2,3)

11 A Rolling Stone introduces himself after good trick (7)

12 Parasite not quite attaching to cows, due to motion (7)

13 Straight part of routine a triumph (4)

14 In brief half–light, stop to catch first bit of warbling — like this? (4,6)

16 See 5

17 With both flanks cleared, swap piece, drawing game (7)

19 Patience perhaps a virtue, having invested time in a girl, foolishly (5,5)

22 Regularly appearing, exam days when school's out (4)

24 Bloke cut metre off plant from Australia (3,4)

25 US city airport not closing with start of operations (7)

26 Hello — a greeting interpreted the wrong way (5)

27 Pharaoh getting back scrubbed, hell amid gross depravity (9)

DOWN

1 Tinge out, 0.001kg boxes? Message noted (7,8)

2 Where, perhaps, to buy a barrier for water (5,3)

3 Bitter cold in desert (5)

4 Punt with second payoff (8)

5,16 Picnic, outdoor exercise (4,2,3,4)

6 Nonsense, such extremes entertained by low figure (9)

7 Quickish pace from China, knees gone might you say? (6)

8 Criticism wears down characters — but these really hurt? (6,3,6)

15 Calibrate in a different way regarding micro-organisms (9)

17 Unprincipled behaviour of women, prince snaffling them all (8)

18 Force doctor and staff to join corporation (8)

20 Caper has doctor incarcerated? (6)

21 Quite lovely (6)

23 Quite ugly (5)

Solution see page 266

Set by Arachne

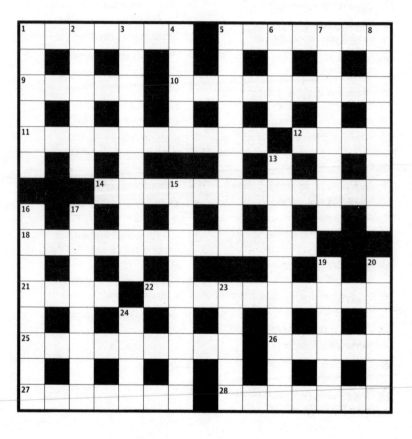

ACROSS

1 More open as a poker player? (7)

5 Stay with the wretched Daniel, say (7)

9 Did butterfly, perhaps, lead to illumination for mystic? (5)

10 Kitty finally got fit in leisure facility (4,5)

11 Mum and daughter collect underwear I dropped and put it on (10)

12 Blue-eyed boy's rebellious action (4)

14 Actor representing genuine class (4,8)

18 Grasses break up topsoil at last, taking ages (5,7)

21 Adolescent's first kiss touching a bit of a nerve (4)

22 Stroke heads of beagles eagerly advancing in anticipation (10)

25 One helping Turkey and half of Uzbekistan start to thrive (9)

26 Conclusion of movie, Three Kings, skirting over inaccuracy (5)

27 Expand section of integral network retrospectively (7)

28 The Spanish shunning sex and food (7)

DOWN

1 Buxom little Maureen's turning into lad (6)

2 Ready for service, nuns gambolled every now and then (6)

3 Amicably finish with girl after 24 hours (10)

4 Regret eating extremely purgative Indian bread (5)

5 Multi-faceted dons exercise and do legal work (9)

6 Curse love, a source of troubled hearts (4)

7 They are frequent visitors, but he is a vagrant (8)

8 Very French attempt to seduce is wrong, legally (8)

13 Yankee puts on silly voice, regardless of what happens (2,3,5)

15 Arachne cries, seized by desire for surge of naughtiness (5,4)

16 Mescal made skipping maidens go up the wall (8)

17 Massive column with rope around (8)

19 I hoard bananas in beehive, perhaps (6)

20 Worships alto and soprano after quarter of an octave (6)

23 Scotsman's armpit bitten by fox terrier (5)

24 Roots of St Ignatius Loyola, soldier and absolutist (4)

Solution see page 267

ACROSS

5 Hang around old president (6)

6 Badly singes rock (6)

9 Composer of Harlem Shuffle (6)

10 Mayor prepared to embrace everyone with a lack of conscience (8)

11 Take off Somerset's first spinner (4)

12 Copper's testimonial is choice (10)

13 Curiously considerate to religious vandalism (11)

18 In a short time a prisoner becomes disloyal (10)

21 Usual time to say goodbye (4)

22 Cut fabric's cost (8)

23 Mounting a revolt (6)

24 Pay a visit for game of cards with the family (4,2)

25 Apron for local tucking into tart (6)

DOWN

1 Break down everything that's sprung up in wood (8)

2 The French slip up and speak angrily (3,3)

3 Showing disrespect in the waterway (8)

4 Half a dozen learned one's facial features (6)

5 Pick up Eliot's suit (6)

7 Marry and relish holding party (6)

8 Burglar's not dangerous, given a wave (4-7)

14 Delighted the European Commission's unchanging (8)

15 Work over would-be enemy (8)

16 Require English to Latin translation (6)

17 Draw back from phone in church (6)

19 King giving order to man (6)

20 Highwayman has power in Italian city (6)

Solution see page 267

Set by Paul

ACROSS

8 Leaning back, a boy exercises a part of the 10 (8)

9,3 Part of the 10 where heavyweight author files page (11)

10 Critical moment on coming to this floating toilet (4)

11 Sexes, perhaps, mate in Germany's capital city (10)

12 First of month welcomed by priests, old feast day (6)

14 Intensively study part of the 10 for spiked plates (8)

15 Consider clamping journalist on a part of the 10 (7)

17 Paul coming backwards, couple come together (7)

20,24 Part of the 10 the norm, that is unlikely to be scalped (8,4)

22 Cake gone — and most of whiskey (6)

23 Drunk ignores pub, feeling better for it? (8,2)

24 See 20

25 Foul eating starter of turkey, cover meat with fat (5)

26 Part of the 10, like that cushioning a blow (8)

DOWN

1 Current measure, degree up with furious exercising? (8)

2 Curse once wrapped up in bandages (4)

3 See 9

4 Unsound notion, as a member reported? (7)

5 In May, county transfixed by a spirit (8)

6 Extra bits in box, belt and buckle finally hauled up (5,5)

7 Beastly lot has little time to get a closer look (4,2)

13 Apparently tough poser is never really understood, maybe initially impossible? (2,8)

16 Rubbish is learnt going places? (8)

18 Church concerned with familiar city in part of the 10 (8)

19 Brilliance breaking through for Britain at war? (7)

21 A private's ending in the army, a simple form of life (6)

22 Wood in, heart out (6)

24 Bread 10 (4)

Solution see page 267

ACROSS

8 Bring up blood containing tiny bit of gallstone after not finishing food (8)

9 England's fifth king stopping imposter's retreat (6)

10 Wally's relative? (4)

11 Saint prepared to fulfil task in shop (10)

12 Awkward lad capturing unfulfilled ladies' hearts (6)

14 Vehicle carrying crop is badly drawn (8)

15 Sack attendant nursing ailment (7)

17 Margin containing recipe associated with English root vegetable (7)

20 Dish out pies cooked by daughter new to the Home Counties (8)

22 Angelica root included in runny centre of spicy sesame paste (6)

23 Research by American leaving sign for social worker in place to eat (10)

24 End of barrel? (4)

25 Fish served with starters of egg mayonnaise for doctor (6)

26 A saint leaving tipsy priest provided with drink (8)

DOWN

1 Cook given a so-called award for pasta (8)

2 Articles about walls of Gulliver's city (4)

3 Tense little boy is difficult to handle (6)

4 One leaving latticework erected in sink (7)

5 Twilight of the Gods depicted in cloth over holy book (8)

6 Tea (and most of its value) produced for ducal mansion (10)

7 Note found by lake in a supernatural place (6)

13 Limitless poteen found in apostles' pants and overalls (10)

16 Drinks to setter's game (3,5)

18 One German-American author was a genius (8)

19 Leader of Georgian separatists means to escape (3,4)

21 Nice mansion, home to comic superhero (6)

22 Rope carried by private therapist (6)

24 Unforeseen hitch involving lid of brown sauce (4)

Solution see page 268

ACROSS

8 Girl finding Vauxhall, say, and Oval on the 26, perhaps? (8)

9 Native American, old and wise (5)

10 See 2

11 Barking noted with terminus in Upminster, best Underground station (4,6)

12 One asking Paddington, say, to eat horse (6)

14 Legendary bull's home pumped with oxygen thus, as preservative (8)

15 First of trains passing through Monument as a rule (7)

17 Appear clumsy in golf with a wedge, ending in bush (7)

20,24 Both end with Underground in Barking (5,3,4)

22 Temple, a resident there is welcomed in by father (6)

23 Master of creativity, heart rate around about a hundred (3,7)

24 See 20

25 For example, Nobel prizes we deigned to accept (5)

26 Duke of Wellington at Waterloo, one ahead of a sovereign (8)

DOWN

1 Plain, fine letters sent in the post (8)

2,10 Black eye initially violet, forming bruise on skin (4,4)

3 Feller's call to take leadership from merchant bankers in Bank (6)

4 Poor white American taking wine with spoon (7)

5 Climber from Stanmore going down the tube (8)

6 Airbrush out borders in removing Pennsylvania city (10)

7 Bored, it's suggested? Take down Waterloo (6)

13 Might granny shove off? (3,7)

16 Flyer values monitors and adjusts a chemical (8)

18 Particular doctor painted on canvas, primarily (8)

19 Workers' home in High Barnet? (7)

21 Flood is over the grass (6)

22 Crime, good and exciting (6)

24 Error on the tube, perhaps? (4)

Solution see page 268

Set by Arachne

To mark a 70th anniversary

ACROSS

1,5,9 Corrupt "haves" all at once inherit our greatest public asset (8,6,7)

10 People in court to condemn Jeremy Hunt neglecting the sick (7)

11 First to admire Mr Aneurin Bevan, our revolutionary 5 reformer? (5)

12 Be rude about 'Arry, chap with scalpel (9)

13 Rebellious 1 5 9 donning uniforms with singular irritability (12)

17 Allocated by month: care reduced, deadlines trashed (12)

20 Pain of north European country losing monarch (9)

22 Theatre cancelling 50% of surgical procedures (5)

23 Current wife describing time in MRI machines? (7)

24 "Skint!", one dental nurse said monotonously (7)

25 Require extremely large hypodermic? (6)

26 Available drug seized by frantic matrons (2,6)

DOWN

1 Regularly sneers at poor old counsellor (6)

2 Hospital study following Bert's last suture (6)

3 Rusting, lidless box hid a can containing nothing (9)

4 Ensure bandage moved lower (8,5)

6 Superior neighbour sounded weird (5)

7 Are still taking pulse, for example of Flora (4,4)

8 Barbarians entertaining very French lady after game (8)

10 Right now I fib about blood group, for good reason (13)

14 Sat at home twirling surgical instrument (9)

15 10 new non-invasive procedures advanced the study of feet (8)

16 American stops small community rejecting very bad treatment (3-5)

18 Attempt to raise spirits of Irishman with case of champagne (6)

19 One behind the other in Accident & Emergency (6)

21 Local London football team spurned by Poles (5)

Solution see page 268

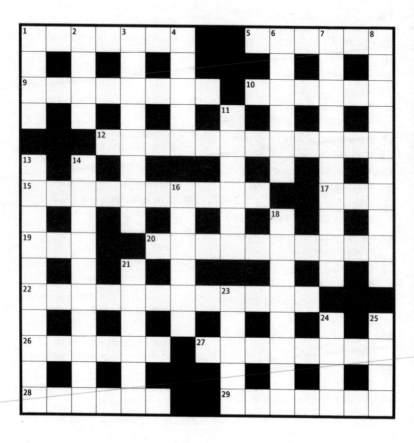

ACROSS

1 Make submissive burglars do this (5,2)

5 Treated mercifully, padre's converted (6)

9 Eccentrics with empty tins for scraps (8)

10 Fail to catch American wife (6)

12 Tool for hard labour damaged hedge in prison (12)

15 Too far away from the mountains? (3,2,5)

17 Whopper claimed when odds are ignored (3)

19 Yank backing good German (3)

20 Unseen cats desperate for nourishment (10)

22 Seeing French dicky birds (12)

26 Artist's materials are not commonly found in the outskirts of Paris (6)

27 One coming out on top — one with a carriage (8)

28 Extremely entertaining gentleman offering drink (6)

29 Advice ignored by the risk-averse woman of property? (7)

DOWN

1 Drug left in London area (4)

2 Tips? Tips from eastern diners (4)

3 Don't part with remaining traffic sign (4,4)

4 Famous saw (5)

6 First mate crossing border (6)

7 Like men, gerbils stray (10)

8 Confused police officer's given command (10)

11 Hornblower's first crew measure up? (6)

13 Dish providing home with constant energy (7,3)

14 Incredible male with ginger snap (10)

16 Nubia's false god (6)

18 Movement of water round wet rocks (8)

21 Couple of punches beginning to count (3-3)

23 Minor country almost heading for disaster (5)

24 Sailor's last in large ship (4)

25 Musical chairs without wings (4)

Solution see page 269

Set by Chifonie

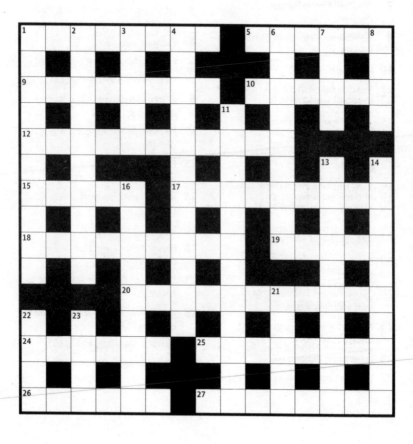

ACROSS

1 Initially see little fellow working for a very small amount (8)

5 Recall breaking into storeroom (6)

9 Muslim unhappy in gym for fencing (8)

10 Cooks for the crew aboard ship (6)

12 Discontinue speech for refreshment (11)

15 Some dog rescuers become monsters (5)

17 American photo taken in Israel produces scepticism (9)

18 The miners adapted to join closely together (9)

19 Half-heartedly incapacitate an aristocrat (5)

20 Boxing promoter in the waste business? (5,6)

24 Disagreement following publicity that's aimless (6)

25 Man returned to island unattached (8)

26 Insect can escape (6)

27 Let's list components? That's most unmoving! (8)

DOWN

1 Wonderful boy in charge, travelling very fast (10)

2 Explain being angry about sovereign's desire (10)

3 Device for soldier's way of working (5)

4 Traveller's joy seeing damn bad loser upset (3,4,5)

6 Development in old conflict (9)

7 Barren meadow needs a bit of nitrate (4)

8 Trick queen over exploit (4)

11 Fail to understand girl has article on train (4,3,5)

13 Question son's disguise in sleazy bar (10)

14 Stop and notice people getting tons of affection (10)

16 Left USSR wrongly supporting Soviet leader? That's worrying! (9)

21 Top swimmer receives ten cents (5)

22 Conflict Mike finds heated (4)

23 Penny has fish? I ask you! (4)

Solution see page 269

63 Set by Imogen

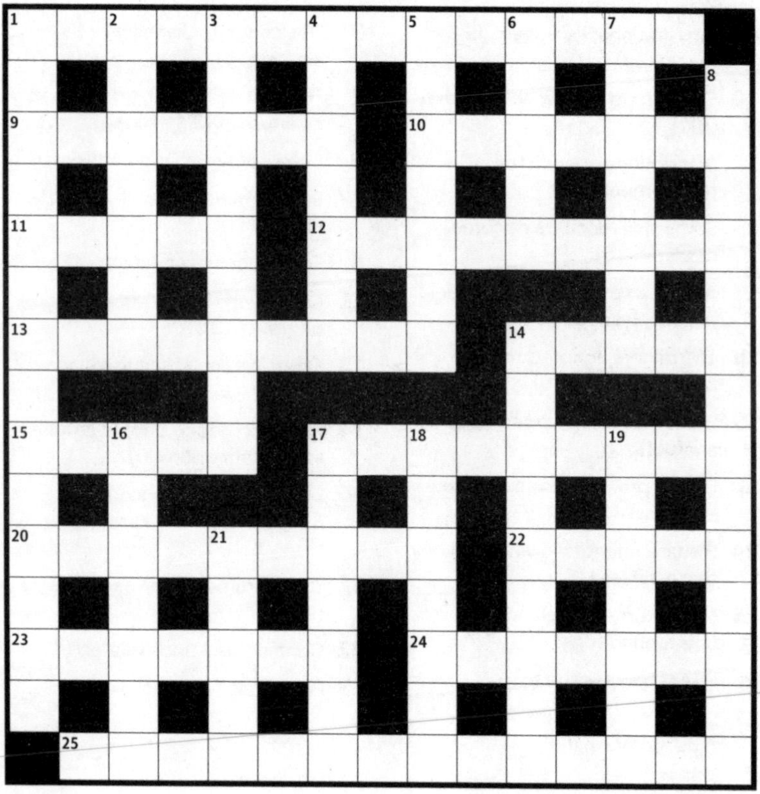

ACROSS

1 Victorian chimney sweeping, an example of nepotism? (4,3,3,4)

9 One way to be dead drunk: swallowing beer at the end (7)

10 Even question being in Europe; from set of data, it's time to leave (7)

11 Box like William, the national hero? (5)

12 Classy old record in handwriting for student of the highest mysteries (9)

13 On short boundary, flyer's not about to go to ground (9)

14 Looking terrified, woman hides in an opening (5)

15 Black bear's pouch (5)

17 Antiquated test hard at elite school, they say (4–5)

20 Intriguing team with new role for Spaniard (9)

22 Battles to unwrap birthday present (5)

23 Dependent on Robin? (7)

24 Falstaff, maybe, here left drinkers' association imbibing special calories (2,5)

25 Wait at priests' table to join them? (4,4,6)

DOWN

1 One that's booked by ref — not good, but he is confused with score (4,3,7)

2 In north–west town finally executing pirate (7)

3 Ditch supporting comic, clarifying this is not peculiar (5,2–2)

4 Have new concerns about defensive position (7)

5 Wooden moves by husband in dance (7)

6 Bravo! Manage to circle Mars (5)

7 Hobby is dreadfully uncivilised (7)

8 Take a breather, others working — I progress spectacularly (4,2,4,4)

14 Primate's one request at first I obey (3,3,3)

16 Curious allure about bachelor, spotted with this (7)

17 Conductor runs in majestically? Not so (7)

18 Tramcar to move, although upset about it (7)

19 Fear losing gold card in house row (7)

21 Go and wash round back of house (5)

Solution see page 269

ACROSS

9 Game to tuck into ale can drunk immediately (2,1,6)

10 Miss America film bags Oscar (5)

11 Inflates price, in the main the wrong way (7)

12 British monarch fed film director (7)

13 Bluer Sierra leaves in summer (5)

14 Bad taste of old booze after hot month (9)

16 Pretty, inspiring love and cheers, twirling with care (15)

19 Reliable music gets son really humming (4,5)

21 In river, you might well see one! (5)

22 Singer's live, unknown in the past (7)

23 A good deal of lawyers make money (7)

24 Feeds girl from the right society (5)

25,3 Pagans first and then ... a US actor? (9,6)

DOWN

1 What gets crazed Turkish big shot around the island (10)

2 Winged creatures in this realm of myriad bats (8)

3 See 25

4 Skin prepared for tattoos (4)

5 Novel to get across entertaining plot in US city (3,7)

6 Aristocrat wanting name for girl (8)

7 Pupils, before English, run late (6)

8 Planned economy holds back ideal state (4)

14 Lacking funds, you do this in hostelry, clearly gutted (10)

15 Leader loudly lamenting Oxford revels (3,7)

17 Possible danger with lighter fluid on stairs (8)

18 What besets politician currently could be stress (8)

20 Showing sadness in bearing, a queen departs (6)

21 Badger to maul tailless equine (6)

22 Ordered something from dodgy drug dealer? (4)

23 English composer's time for recital (4)

Solution see page 270

Set by Brummie

ACROSS

1 Growth-restricted marsupial gets tense before jump (9)

6 Year in prison shade (4)

8 Colouring agent's no good without positive temperature (8)

9 Indication of impact: scattered red dust (6)

10 Complaint of Cruel Sea's debut production (6)

11 Is a ham put out to carve, son? (8)

12 Articles about next Greek deity (6)

15 Experience flu outbreak that's not common (8)

16 USSR in a mess, following pressure from an older European state (8)

19 Work on engine to remove cocaine traces? (6)

21 After drink, rock group has drugs for another group (8)

22 Nameless wild flower (6)

24 Is perversely advanced still (6)

25 Up to date on focus again (8)

26 Refreshment left for bird (4)

27 City game after US guy's comeback (9)

DOWN

1 August: put gold back (5)

2 Pornographic old book site (7)

3 University representative's sad song? (5)

4 Frank, given space, gets ahead (2,5)

5 Act to hold newspapers down (9)

6 Bully with bar on end of rope is a danger to cattle (7)

7 Astonished by one-way fold (9)

13 Quite sour, off colour (9)

14 Aix exploded atomic device, no question about it (9)

17 Stop circling source of Ugandan rivers — it's bizarre! (7)

18 No way drink is medicine! (7)

20 Boasted about name being made regal (7)

22 Minister against electric current saloon? (5)

23 High spot — of English year, that is (5)

Solution see page 270

66

Set by Paul

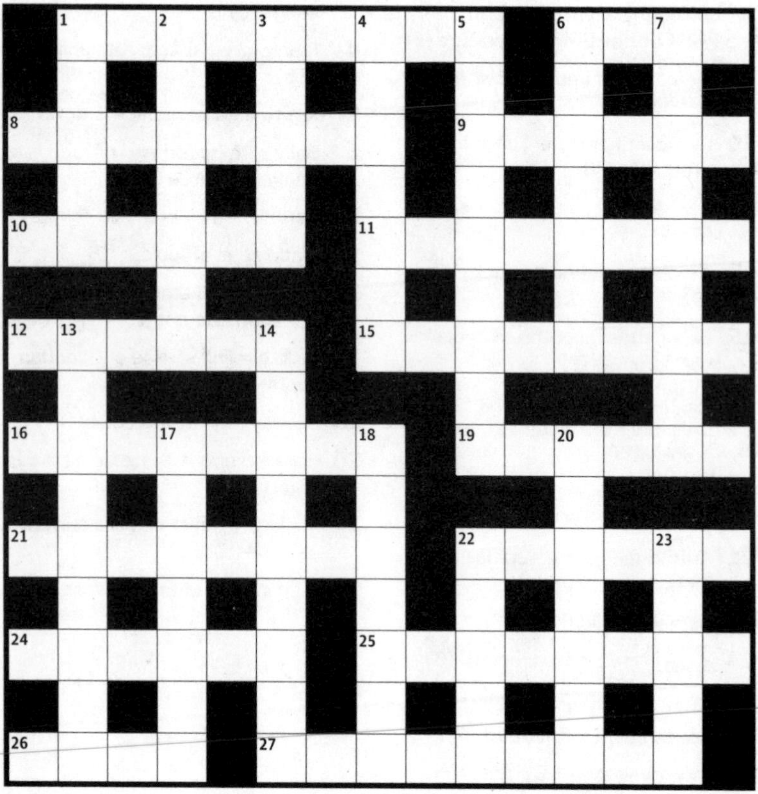

ACROSS

1 Bread Irish pub rejected in place of buns? (4,5)

6 No longer green, somewhat blue? (4)

8 Order prohibited at the last minute (8)

9 Streaks about to happen for artist (6)

10 Three-quarters of men making some fast moves? (3-3)

11 Duty to protect or deliver from evil? (8)

12 Big name almost sure to avoid relegation (4,2)

15 Arrest in Australian newspaper written about, seedy American thing (8)

16 Cover featuring stunner, smeared (8)

19 Fears, Caribbean style? (6)

21 Children's book in minor novel (3,5)

22,1down Somewhere in Brighton where I sunbathed audaciously, catching cold (6,5)

24 Country — one hosting race at its centre (6)

25 Not entirely equipped to host opera that's unusual (8)

26 Subject of selfie repeatedly in shared image (4)

27 US comedienne possibly not scratching old bottom (9)

DOWN

1 See 22 across

2 Hot meal without starter in fish (7)

3 Crow going over a Portuguese city (5)

4 Hazard floating in crosses initially, winger ascendant (7)

5 Held man had to cover up something shady (9)

6 Book on old server, reportedly? (7)

7 Wee, around 568ml? (4-5)

13 Body part malodorous, black in colour (5,4)

14 Succeed in pronouncing fanciful name of Russian hen? (4,2,3)

17 Dubai, say — Uncle Sam finally losing it (7)

18 Rat den I set alight (7)

20 Back 'urdler, say, champion (7)

22 Norse goddess UN leader once exalted (5)

23 Small handle for beam (5)

Solution see page 270

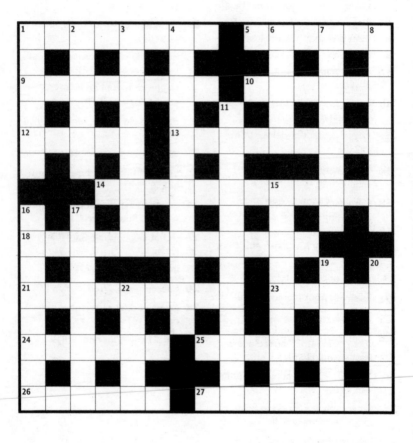

ACROSS

1 Become annoyingly amorous — we object going: " _____ " (3,1,4)

5 Singer's keeping last of home comforts (6)

9 Removed Dexter, retired hurt (8)

10 Eager to fight Rod and Henry in turn (4-2)

12 Stop working in centre of Beaune — I'm getting outta here! (5)

13 Eat in low spirits, extremely low spirits (9)

14 In replay, clatters dopy old wingers (12)

18 Criminal's old mate wrong — 10 isn't being clobbered (12)

21 Plan succeeded with huge cutting back (9)

23 Writer's book is out around second half of the month (5)

24 Flash Gordon, flyer (6)

25 Has new single out — it's dirty (8)

26 Open Dad's wine (6)

27 Best saying 12 at start? That's unexpected! (2,6)

DOWN

1 Blasted cat's bitten tot — that's upsetting (6)

2 Juicy piece of news — time it proved effective (6)

3 Narrator describes sport he wants you to join (9)

4 Again Emperor's given order — Congress won't be restricted by it (4,8)

6 On top of one-time beauty — she's fascinating (5)

7 Sweetheart's a joy — short but a really good looker (5,3)

8 Director Nick has succeeded in style, but not content (8)

11 Hard cash? Yes and no (7,5)

15 Criticise cold wine scandal? (9)

16 Made a mistake — came clean after changing gender (6,2)

17 Politicians here — most are reportedly not Labour (8)

19 Found in Waterstone's, the right book (6)

20 Nervous performing at the Fringe? (2,4)

22 Cross, tense and nearly going nuts (5)

Solution see page 271

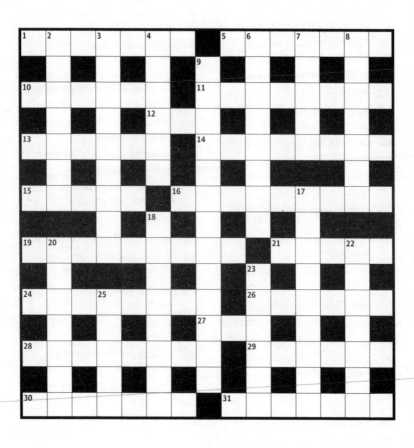

ACROSS

1 Huit cargo? (7)

5 Students, upset by low grade, now rioting at the end of the day (7)

10 I see handle turned by superhero (6)

11 In general, small clothes (8)

12 Weapon £1,000? Nice one! (3)

13 Caught taking back Silver, our cat (6)

14 Multiplied total? Sounds horrible (8)

15 Cheat bridge partners, each with king (5)

16 Profitable spring's exhausted (4,5)

19 Craft beers — how? Add a bit of malt (4,5)

21 Bird goes wild protecting egg (5)

24 Roman Catholic's revolted by online sins and splits (8)

26 "Magician" Messi evades Ronaldo's lunges in netting headers (6)

27 Favourite jumper (3)

28 Maverick provides show? False (8)

29 Fruit prepared over cooker (6)

30 Cocaine found in tea, right? It's not true (7)

31 Fools subdue good man with taunts (7)

DOWN

2 US mammal managed to inhale cold carbon dioxide? (7)

3 Come in, I'm travelling both ways with great excitement (9)

4 Adult leaves country with longing (6)

6 American lorry emptied after fuel spill in practical way (8)

7 Martin and James, as heads of school? (5)

8 Fellow left to turn into female monster (7)

9 Stuttering woe produced by this? (6-7)

17 Cor! Parent in the making? (9)

18 Vegetable producer (8)

20 Sea creature Spooner has around 4? (7)

22 Isn't busy good queen bee? (7)

23 Politician enters No 10 with special European charge (6)

25 Privet trimmed unusually as a snake (5)

Solution see page 271

Set by Imogen

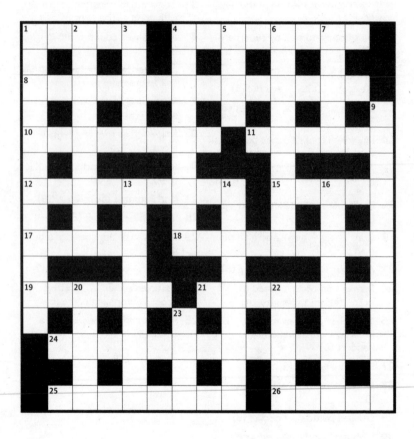

ACROSS

1 Rock room, turning away leader of criminals (2,3)

4 Together in firm, the lower classes fawned around one (8)

8 One may help police drag men off, keeping peace at first between two women (6,8)

10 Flirts with right-winger, getting one animated (3,5)

11 Racists bearing cross round as warning (6)

12 What Piaf had indoors at intervals — waders (2,7)

15 Take part of sheet (the bottom) and stick back (5)

17 Tucking into acorns? At first you are allowed to (5)

18 Record holder's go on board (9)

19 Two or three prepositions, altogether (2,4)

21 Strong feelings leading to hard argument — over its expansion? (8)

24 Dangerous creature in trap? Rubbish — fright that is for nothing (3,4,7)

25 I say Anna is a cow (8)

26 Gardeners stand nervously around spades? Not very (5)

DOWN

1 Timid hangman trembles, needing utmost strength (5,3,4)

2 Bishop forces sports fans abroad (5,4)

3 Hard work is great in service? On the contrary (5)

4 "Democrat in, Tories out!" — that is to confuse (9)

5 Start to cut, shape and grind (4)

6 Old king's service perhaps about to save the pound (9)

7 I fight to seize Republican ground (5)

9 To be clear, on planets not our own there is no opening for life (2,5,5)

13 Being possible to reach, successfully phone restaurant (3-2-4)

14 Hear master had a seizure, having overindulged (9)

16 Purple with fresh air and bungee jumping (9)

20 Tennis's beginning on grass in a moment (5)

22 Murdered, throat cut — get the law! (5)

23 Inspiration taken from heraldic lion (4)

Solution see page 271

ACROSS

1 Recurrent saying in busy pubs? (7,2)

6 Oddly shunned, said piteous goodbye (5)

9 Suffuse disrobed limbs with beginnings of unalloyed eroticism (5)

10 Consummate marriage? Not so! (9)

11 Accommodation and clothing denied to French revolutionary over time (4-1-5)

12 Filthy place ultimately became eyesore (4)

14 Conveyance of gas round back of Number 10 (7)

15 Spooner's fake history published on the internet (7)

17 Port went off, in a manner of speaking (7)

19 Quietly handle extremely rare love potion (7)

20 Left-wingers in Italian towns campaigned hard and long (4)

22 Are responsible for Her Majesty meeting Blue Peter dog in private (10)

25 Where Communists alone are elected to run neonatal facility (9)

26 Drug finally injected into bare elbow (5)

27 Decent sandwiches start to entice relative (5)

28 Depend on Jane name-dropping without ostentation (9)

DOWN

1 First to burst flaccid balloon (5)

2 Present for discussion on second key food additive (5,4)

3 Gracious Evita reportedly turned up to embrace workers (10)

4 Collage of Matisse showing least variation (7)

5 A supporter of mine (3,4)

6 Pain of brill swallowing tip of hook (4)

7 Sluggish ferrets regularly found beneath home (5)

8 Draw peacekeepers' fire with high explosive (9)

13 Maiden, with tact, ordered entree (10)

14 Alliance of nearly everybody in Congress (9)

16 Turn red, sat awkwardly on top with a leg on each side (9)

18 Criminal cartel headed by leader of pheasant pluckers (7)

19 Surreptitiously photograph your American manuscript (7)

21 Memory of country singer on the radio (5)

23 Each is ruefully discontented after night before (5)

24 Old boyfriend said to be member of orchestra (4)

Solution see page 272

ACROSS

1 Just emission from drinker, perhaps, during recent setback (7)

5 On filling casks, press these for attention (7)

9 Magnate's boozer with no counter (5)

10 Churlish grin that passes between supporters in house (5-4)

11 High spirits, as sexy Hubert dances unclothed (10)

12 Fish, which aren't sampled (4)

14 It proceeds by degrees in Lee's classic US novel, with one small exception (7,5)

18 Spare house in Westminster — trendy 9 enjoyed it (12)

21 Day and month avoided by judge, when appropriate (4)

22 Surly git, 'e's playing at this time of year? (4,6)

25 Amended religious lesson, dry in newer version (9)

26 Perfunctory gift (5)

27 Gaunt and small with sharp features (7)

28 Bind wife in portable seat (7)

DOWN

1 Turn up identical notes containing pound symbol (6)

2 Not having enough soft down, presumably (4,2)

3 Re dance, I'll be transformed! (10)

4 Stretch fabric covers of lively colour given top rating (5)

5 Groups of readers for whom Spooner's chef sheds tears? (4,5)

6 Undertaking pilot's last request (4)

7 Basic liability for firm shot on court (8)

8 A few decline to support region's top cricket team (8)

13 It's paradise, newly created without Eden's first plant (10)

15 Nimble American operative taking both sides in (9)

16 Country has guards roaming round (8)

17 Ruin agent set up by subordinate (8)

19 Son ungrammatically accepted bet (6)

20 Royal nipper's right to ascend (6)

23 Refusal accepted by broadcaster, going back a long time (5)

24 Partial problem in German dynasty (4)

Solution see page 272

72 Set by Paul

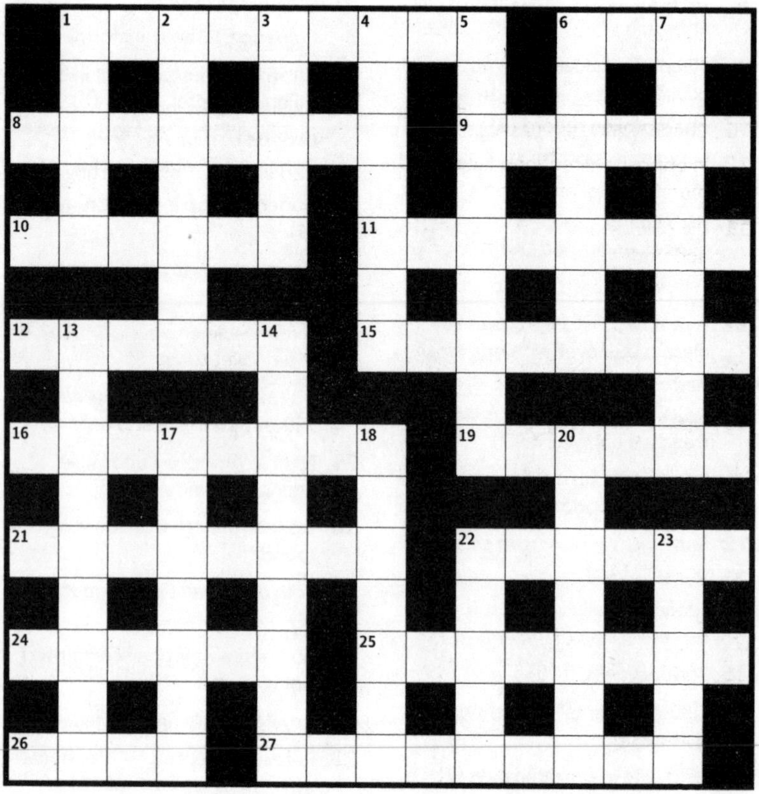

ACROSS

1 Cup — runner holds it during service (9)

6 Hit — almost hit back (4)

8 Voices raised in terrible argument, referee initially knocked over by players (8)

9 Capital idea to start with, after one's broken record (6)

10 In opposite directions, lacquered metalware taken (6)

11 Big college that is accommodating unknown number (4-4)

12 See 19

15 Jumper in equestrian sport with narrow margin of victory (4,4)

16 Glassy expression's first seen in very upset suitor (8)

19,12 Electrical device — more foolish instrument of punishment (6,6)

21 Southern frontiersman, big chap (8)

22 Feed unlimited dill, in herbaceous plant (6)

24 Car from Providence somewhere in Italy (6)

25 Hunter, head in plaster bloodied on a rock (8)

26 Sponge cakes right for composer (4)

27 Most happening to see border in Italian city that's not closed (9)

DOWN

1 King spoiling absurd plan (5)

2 Sailor finds companion on piece of land (7)

3 See 23

4 Gun crime at a higher level getting criticism initially (5-2)

5 English books inclined to be involved (9)

6 Red skirts — rip off skirting (7)

7 Compound of zinc's the cure in the end for German intellect (9)

13 Variety in a wine list a growing concern for heavy drinkers, perhaps? (9)

14 Evidence hack, say, was there to find clue — nothing concerning promotion in it (9)

17 See 22

18 Greek song others performed around piano (7)

20 With drunken glee I'm glugging absinthe to begin with — how far gone? (7)

22,17 Scanning text quickly, Twitter covering fear of urinals? (5,7)

23,3 Ride straight on up the creek (5,5)

Solution see page 272

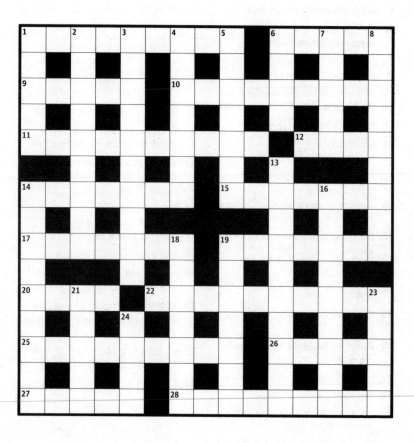

ACROSS

1 Policeman seizes haul in fortified house (4,5)

6 Doctor keeps Victorian pickup quiet (5)

9 Mature scripture writer (5)

10 Marty sees problem in instalment plan (4,5)

11 Broken chairs in the way here by the Irish Sea (10)

12 Stern parent (4)

14 Even a place of higher education has class (7)

15 Former partner modelled naked (7)

17 Charlie gets poorer daily (7)

19 Function where Hazel meets man (7)

20 Be sorry about daughter being discourteous (4)

22 Distress character reversing jalopy (10)

25 Love Bill's speech (9)

26 A sign tooth decay hasn't started (5)

27 Mollycoddle girl in US city (5)

28 Uncouth set slates building (9)

DOWN

1 Supernatural being left in danger (5)

2 Thoughtful when supporting old dear (9)

3 Model worker gets a rise or equivalent (10)

4 King involved in crash in Wales (7)

5 Bookstore? (7)

6 Man put away wife (4)

7 Compact found in Battersea (5)

8 Cast aspersions on circle embarrassed over sex appeal (9)

13 Old writers echo identical passwords (4,6)

14 Centaur in trouble? That's doubtful! (9)

16 Subordinate holds fruit for the men of the family (5,4)

18 One is pragmatic about an inclination (7)

19 Complaint when Lawrence beat American (7)

21 Fuzz arresting ringleader in swamp (5)

23 Lapdogs harbour small bugs (5)

24 Suspicious of conflict over youth leader (4)

Solution see page 273

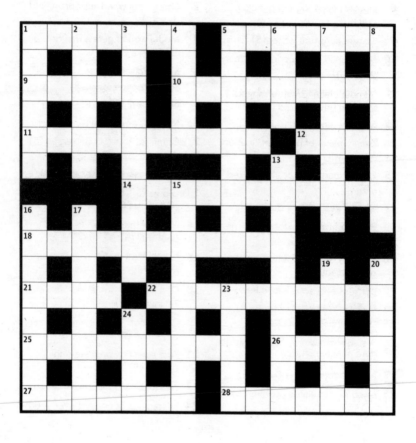

ACROSS

1 What contentious folk often get for seconds? (5,2)

5 Miserly investment in worthy sculpture, for instance (4,3)

9 Is rubbish put back in trunks? (5)

10 Get dirty, menacing look after party (9)

11 "Almost clean" Brexit arranged, that can be delivered (10)

12 Painter's energy always returns (4)

14 Wild animal with truer colour (11)

18 Rein in twins, those running the enterprise (11)

21 What Jersey did, presumably, banning English humour (4)

22 Whistleblower runs, busy and able to change direction (10)

25 Grouse when main road's used the wrong way — playing ball! (9)

26 Audacious League of Nations enterprise originally unsupported (5)

27 Here at sea might one see son strip off? (7)

28 Bent journalist beyond suspicion (7)

DOWN

1 British state's contribution to continental breakfast? (6)

2 Minister's canny, calling in the artillery (6)

3 Music from Southern religious ceremonies? (10)

4 Here we go for relief — relief coming up in stages (5)

5 Barrage's fluid seal broken (9)

6 Gas, once found, regularly discharged (4)

7 A game soldier first to attempt a written defence (8)

8 Cow with last of clover to chew coming in later (8)

13 Any child is mad giving pound for a necklace (5,5)

15 Characteristic craft revolutionised nameless country (9)

16 Charming qualities masking Nutmeg's ugly looks (8)

17 In Montmartre, a joint seldom found (8)

19 Put paid to king, moving bishop not pawn (6)

20 Top husband in contest getting promotion (6)

23 Punster's last to cut gag (5)

24 This is oddly coloured (4)

Solution see page 273

ACROSS

8 Revealing backside reportedly, kiss partner first? (8)

9 Useless dad not taken seriously at first (5)

10 Pass over waste container (4)

11 Wind far, all wrapped up in swelling burst of energy (5,5)

12 Furniture item solver suggested? (6)

14 Penning notes on passing back, handyman defender (8)

15 Deepest part of script in story likely to crumble (7)

17 Prowler, male part on parade, initially (7)

20 Music in middle of performance, played at centre (8)

22 Drink carrier (6)

23 Standard for Morgan perhaps, happy fellow (5,5)

24,24down Gloria Gaynor's first and last gig? (8)

25 That's one place to go, briefly (2,3)

26 Together in print and embossed (2,6)

DOWN

1 Tie spoon on last (8)

2 Cricketer in female underwear (4)

3 Problem with smalls filling up well (6)

4 Whip under the nether regions, as virago (7)

5 Treat Peter to a Trial by Jury, say? (8)

6 Touring Berlin, take nipper (5-5)

7 Girl riding without support (6)

13 Server you rolled up, on which a source of milk and bread (3,7)

16 Cut tatting speed? (8)

18 Foreign students having secured top grade, time for cheers (8)

19 Publisher taking initiative originally in shooting writer? (7)

21 Knickers ultimately abandoned, sounds about right — for this? (6)

22 Individual opening individual correspondence (6)

24 See 24 across

Solution see page 273

76

Set by Brummie

ACROSS

8 Lock fixer and musical stagehand (8)

9 Pam too slack for graft (6)

10 Put in a good word for Seal (4)

11 Young producer, calculating type (10)

12 Gear pin hindrance? Not quite (6)

14 "Weird things" — state in which stars may be seen (5,3)

15 Clotho's from south Middlesex location? (7)

17 "Iodine in gin's a stimulant" — Tramp (7)

20 Star's debut appearance in daily soap? (8)

22 Fly at an early age (6)

23 Vehicle 101 has complete lack of data that produces growth (10)

24 Brook's headless fish (4)

25 Kind of heathen, one to be avoided (6)

26 Cynic died before seeing about having a ball (8)

DOWN

1 Irk privileged American pest (4,4)

2 Medic wants silver for headache (4)

3 Unit's music award not quite the ultimate in prestige (6)

4 Stone-like work by a band (7)

5 Bounder's pet? (8)

6 Discontented Salzburg to restrict shopping venue? Fine — no big deal (5,5)

7 Band's run exposed (6)

13 Spiky catkins, say, found in the American Midwest (6,4)

16 German city with little time to turn up distinctive qualities (8)

18 Burn unseen, as sculptor under sun (8)

19 Soldiers providing vessel support via radio (7)

21 President's view of newspaper? (6)

22 Mo has present for an unimportant person (6)

24 River fish's swim (4)

Solution see page 274

77

Set by Qaos

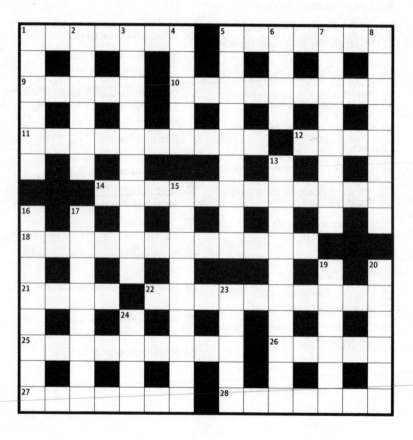

ACROSS

1 Pollock and other fish numbers returning (7)

5,26 Actor producing a cliche in a state (7,5)

9 Since I wear layers, it's more cold (5)

10 Promenades that are out of this world (9)

11 Cable binds black line after home's impossible to conquer (10)

12 Nothing evil in short book? (4)

14 Squeeze right into ship where hacks might be found (5,7)

18 Joy for old Benn is without end: people oust leader! (12)

21 I career around, then collapse (4)

22 Unorthodox final position of Humpty Dumpty? (3,3,4)

25 Spoiled cat: "I loved the good life" (5,4)

26 See 5

27 Always in favour of First Lady (Republican) (7)

28 Welcome tale from the past (7)

DOWN

1 Legless man, one goes into pub to participate (4,2)

2 Badger picks up virus No 5 within city limits (6)

3 Season and turn Chinese food (6,4)

4 Clouds rising from Maghrib mines (5)

5 Film work on a second job (9)

6 Allegedly, media mogul's a hood (4)

7 Revised bible held by a theologian's all made up (2–6)

8 Armageddon might take a while? (4,4)

13 Prepare clues for Everyman to begin with, Sunday lights up (10)

15 Tailor cries over Trump becoming more untidy (9)

16 Remove dish to fridge (3,3,2)

17 Time after time, I shall get the queen in sensational film (8)

19 Boxer carries cold, firm cloth (6)

20 Feeling tired, Mole takes shelter (6)

23 Train tickets over 85% off per person (5)

24 Fuel stored in older vehicles (4)

Solution see page 274

ACROSS

7 Writer like Nelson? (9)

8 Substitute for axes (5)

9 1000 + 1 + 50 + 0 + 50? It's about a unit (9)

10 Measure direction using sound (5)

12 He's a priest, surrounded by noise (6)

13 At position in A&E wanting 6 (8)

16 CD music made poorly, lacking special energy (7)

19 Backtrack with Poles moving in ... (7)

22 ... one agrees for fool to come in (8)

25 Co-pilot finally completes putting fuel over nose of Boeing (6)

27 Youngsters left inside discos (5)

28 Be 51 stone in front, without odd tummy (9)

29 Delivered my first line? (5)

30 Perfect summer month for record drink (4,5)

DOWN

1 I dine out after 10 (6)

2 EU's regret over drug (8)

3 In wind, I umpire inside (6)

4 Answer parsed cryptically and placed far apart (7)

5 Important old city fellow (6)

6 O'Grady in orthodox drag to make endings funny (6)

11 Terminate Sierra, Romeo, Quebec, Papa? (4)

14 See 16

15 Earl with posh car? Perhaps this is to be human (3)

16,14 100 locks for furniture (6)

17 Democrat very upset by party's old computer system (3)

18 Capable of two thirds output? That's dodgy (2,2)

20 No prize? I'm to receive 2nd cup (8)

21 As football team loses a league, 1 to 100 (7)

23 S-setter retired to tour the capital of Latvia (6)

24 Er ... er ... twice the amount of hesitation (6)

25 Toy eaten up by Lord Wolf (6)

26 Praised young Miliband after his elevation, say (6)

Solution see page 274

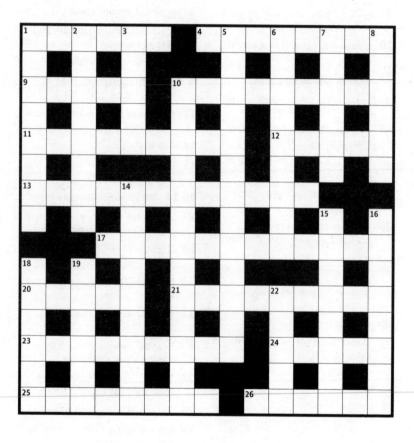

ACROSS

1 Geriatric's party I'm a bit annoyed about (6)

4 Landowner introducing married daughter was embarrassed (8)

9 Finish job in WC and look embarrassed (5)

10 Travelling kings were sticking together, one might say (9)

11 Forged bill in M&S or Aldi, say, a source of irritation (9)

12 Slight setback hampering European policies (5)

13 Fashion etc, the Tudors extended (12)

17 After study, no women find time for revision (12)

20 Run through museum unclothed, ending in shop (3,2)

21 Abandoned rebel leader probed by secret police (4,5)

23 Order to confine gangster for last two members of panel (9)

24 Single global enterprise returned early deposit (5)

25 Without us, Oedipus Rex collapsed — shock treatment applied (8)

26 Dam with added function, not the conventional sort (6)

DOWN

1 One'll break faith with failing soldiers (8)

2 Those visiting solicitors holding teacher up (8)

3 Airline lady's mounted remedial course (5)

5 Barman, in short, quite contrary to start with (6,7)

6 Individual approaching home with zeal (2,7)

7 Mum wearing extremely leaky overall (6)

8 Study comes to an end, keeping good time (6)

10 No Etonian detected at USA gathering? (5-8)

14 Inscrutable type — he's quiet during lean times (3,6)

15 He'll judge about six sheep, first in ring (8)

16 Mobile characters in Tate don't care for? (6,2)

18 Loose car part regularly fixed in hour by champ (6)

19 Nutmeg's stopping show in German city (6)

22 Beyond a double bend, river's clear blue (5)

Solution see page 275

80

Set by Crucible

ACROSS

1 Artist William's crazy giving up whiskey (7)

5 Greek poet's energy about to inspire one of her letters (7)

10 See 27

11 Suffering disease, charge 1's applicator (10)

12 A turn in northern waters? (6)

13 Rice stirred with milk, a speciality of 22 10 (8)

14 1's supporter savages parasite (9)

16 German agent turned Yankee traveller (5)

17 Left in dilemma, as was Gloucester in 27 10 (5)

19 Conservative US campus backed dead judge (9)

23 He's temporarily transferred function on river (8)

24 Rejected 22 10 for one prize (6)

26 Beatles (two) see boss (4,4,2)

27,10 Disliking learning about play (4,4)

28 Disrupt current London theatre offensive (7)

29 Target revolutionary in service in 27 10's state (7)

DOWN

2 Oriental artwork embargo in furniture shop (7)

3 Good singers have large chests (5)

4 Start of major scheme in Italy needs graft (7)

6 A tortuous maths problem involving tubes (6)

7 Picture beam blocking entrance (9)

8 Vets less quiet bugs (7)

9 Fit guy, about 40, with a fashion magazine in city (3-2-8)

15 Laird's way to acquire county with river (9)

18 Told story about restricting wife's rest (3-4)

20 First of clues (1 across) nearly upset island (7)

21 Shades cover personnel facilities (7)

22 27 initially engendered conflict between daughters (6)

25 Come round with a Scotsman (5)

Solution see page 275

81

Set by Imogen

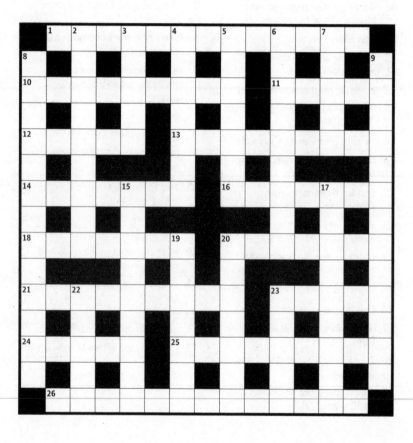

ACROSS

1 In scientific study trip miss coach; pity! (6,7)

10 Engineers new fabulous figures for property lists (4,5)

11 Old mnemonic device a joke at university (5)

12 Legume, very hot, to eat with the others ... (5)

13 ... guy has a way to avoid legume (9)

14 Force that turns English out at a yard in town (7)

16 Where one may read the news, telling of traffic congestion (7)

18 Led astray and misused a month back (7)

20 Time went fast, they say; it's sickening (4,3)

21 Cell for one on the staff, briefly, at Oxford college (9)

23 Needle, say, reversed to make lace (3,2)

24 Hesiod is truly entertaining poet (5)

25 Male deadlier when swinging the hammer here (6,3)

26 Chap in key wager collapses complex mathematical construction (10,3)

DOWN

2 Showing a slight tinge, metal smoked, keeping temperature well up (9)

3 Graphically transform most of pain relief (5)

4 Lying undisturbed at first in peaceful state (7)

5 Cry of joy as overweight girl takes on husband (7)

6 Appropriate person looking for most prosperous area of the country? (9)

7 Punch hole in cloth (5)

8 Grunt, adjusting corset — it's no business of the state! (7,6)

9 "Pooch! That sweet sauce!", as Spooner might do well to say (3,3,7)

15 So great a number deprived of noble title? (9)

17 This on table in diner on Level 5 (9)

19 Top of loft in the morning frozen up: that's beside the point (7)

20 During drinking bout, large mixer (7)

22 India feeds pest with a cucumber preparation (5)

23 Sow chews end of one waistcoat (5)

Solution see page 275

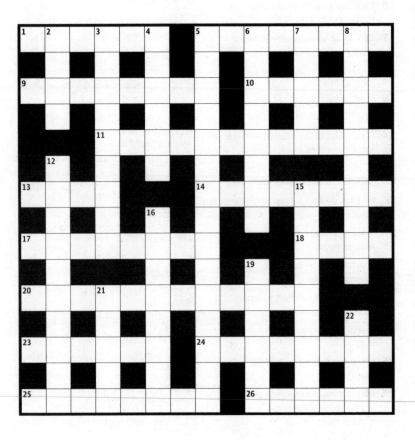

ACROSS

1 Bare-legged, perhaps, avoiding ugly leer of despicable person (3,3)

5 With right to be called, let it end badly (8)

9 Buzzer and horn sound about right for Russian course requirement (8)

10 Press ID (6)

11 Bride can suss out contact information (8,4)

13 Wind and fire wiping out half the network system (2-2)

14 Regularly repair musical instrument's sound receivers (8)

17 Success with other arrangement so far (8)

18 Bias of south-facing gardens (4)

20 High on drugs, ruins the environment (12)

23 This source of insect sounds almost a type of food (6)

24 Willing in the morning to empower (8)

25 Once more fire in nerd-like fashion (8)

26 Internet mob organisation (6)

DOWN

2 Top copy chased by Times (4)

3 Found Basil Faulty in east of France hotel! (9)

4 Bereavement between the covers of gay magazine (6)

5 Perhaps French camping call centre restricted agreement (7,8)

6 Record attempt to cover pole in fabric (8)

7 Subject to choice, but not quite (5)

8 Regularly repair musical instrument's sound amplifier (3,7)

12 Four in cast mutinied, like Piglet (10)

15 Proof of wanton tartiness (9)

16 Anxious heart of Putin: his currency finally devalued (8)

19 South-western enterprise zone vacated in allergic response (6)

21 Man of religion employed by Arab billionaire (5)

22 Type of rock garden looked a mess to begin with (4)

Solution see page 276

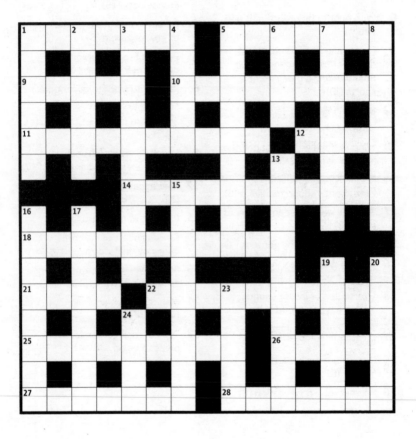

ACROSS

1 See 26

5 Figure needing support about weight (7)

9 Cycling French novelist? Certainly not! (5)

10 See 26

11 Boss wanting a pipe and new shorts (10)

12 Smooth fellow, left-leaning priest (4)

14 Exciting star in music who might use a 27 12? (11)

18 Potentially dodgy stuff in the claret left lechers too sozzled (11)

21 Part of footmark effaced in procession (4)

22 The fourteenth rule overturned wrong score in game (4,6)

25 Maybe menu's split bananas with cereal in (5,4)

26,1,10 Lack coordination to go 100% 27? (2,3,7,3,6)

27 Like modern gadgets? Like everything, almost! (7)

28 Experiences with one unenlightened sect (7)

DOWN

1 Use 1 10 on tender jacket of lace (6)

2 Cameron's in an upset state (6)

3 Sound device in better film, after something corny? (3,7)

4 Military headgear from mum a big hit (5)

5 Daughters in drag come out, showing fair feature (6,3)

6 A fling, one of the Shades of Grey? (4)

7 Least usual alcohol, note, is in champagne (8)

8 Widespread internet application, one aiding relaxation (8)

13 Advance so far up, welcoming spin in vehicle (10)

15 New linen hat worn by a man (9)

16 Lose sports day, having fought (8)

17 Concerned with using 1 10 (8)

19 Where 1 10 are available (2,4)

20 Said why a poor area's accepted protection (6)

23 Nick's ruling out place of worship (5)

24 Used 1 10 on fabric (4)

Solution see page 276

ACROSS

1 Beauty treatment of French origin (Calais, possibly) (7)

5 Let everyone outstanding be audibly spoken (7)

9 Virtue good ... then to relish a version of the Arabian Nights (6,3,6)

10,15 A pair of mice cavorting? Not love at first sight! (5,5)

11 One rescued by flying horseman surrounded by African dromedaries (9)

12 Cutting the roast at first with charm (9)

14 Ezra Pound's heart battered and blue (5)

15 See 10

16 City's to be conquered in the end (4,2,3)

18 In the pipeline, the tons of crude oil initially imported by Arab country being curtailed (3,2,4)

21 Red ground edgy but even (5)

22 Choose the Guardian's first game in case of brief visits (7-4,4)

23 Gratefully received royalty payments (7)

24 Educated and beautiful, finally made some money (7)

DOWN

1 Pedant from start to finish on position by compilers (7)

2 Eccentric kind of rough hustle (10,5)

3 Fall for an item of linen hotel included (9)

4 Australian half-rewritten scripture (5)

5 An EU precursor lavishes love stories (9)

6 Somewhat emotionally upset, it's plain (5)

7 Paced like men of York? (6,2,3,4)

8 Upsetting oath about vessel in unenlightened time (4,3)

13 More calls from the world and his wife (9)

14 Fresh approach covering the ultimate in cookery books (9)

15 What you might need, when at first you spot wasp in apartment (7)

17 Gone ahead, accepting a terrible year with one thing on top of another (7)

19 In a way that's recurring decimal? (5)

20 Sexy amateur role essentially gets praise (5)

Solution see page 276

ACROSS

1 Split up, assuming sex is performed with energy (6)

4 What could be thanks to Shakespeare's tunic (6)

9 Solvers aren't supposed to cheat — that's too much! (3,8,4)

10 Made man disobey restraining order (6)

11 Have a go at it near to engineers (4,4)

12 Firm slice finds corner, say (3,5)

14 One who's drawn Dolly? (6)

15 High-flyer's saucier gyrating, removing last of lingerie (6)

18 Understanding where population's 50+? (8)

21 Box left to transport in the future (8)

22 Inclined to see pole dancing as opening (6)

24 Georgia's proportional representation? (5,10)

25 Frank army holding Western Europe finally (6)

26 Push for reduced charge (6)

DOWN

1 See Green Papers rejected by Home Counties (7)

2 Scene described by Chekhov is tantalising (5)

3 In Berlin, the following entrance is risky (2-2-3)

5 A news organisation of USA covering Liberal issues (7)

6 Not believing it's the CIA complex (9)

7 One following course finds election boring (7)

8 Emptied cocktail over the dress (6)

13 Barking, or place in China (9)

16 A bit like singer's prize (7)

17 European skipping champions (more than one Dutch) (7)

18 Camper director? (6)

19 Windows installer close to updating, not working as hard (7)

20 Current account, in retirement, hidden by trained pilot (7)

23 Stop firsts from LSE, exposing those using phones (3,2)

Solution see page 277

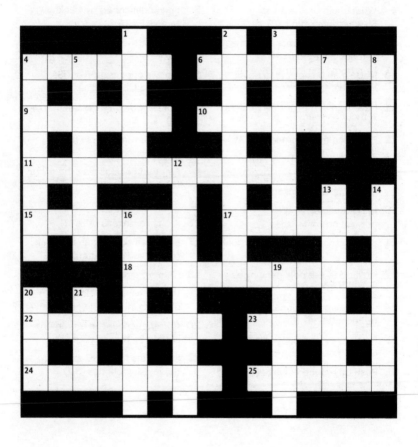

ACROSS

4 Piece left in social system (6)

6,23 Old rule initially in play? (5,3,6)

9 Magic word, in principle, as esoteric (6)

10 Popular old canary (8)

11 First body, you might say, to tour northern French city (11)

15 Fix shower after showering without shower (7)

17 Couplet about — six fewer than this? (7)

18 Place and time to bag an old house (11)

22 Setter noted patterns in reverse (4-4)

23 See 6

24 See 21

25 Basic food in drinking establishment for 2 (6)

DOWN

1 State with a petition in US city (6)

2 Bum seated, a fanatic about to perform (4-3-3)

3 Benefit in payment, evocative (8)

4 Primate and friar (8)

5 Where passengers accommodated cheaply in back of cars, fury among drivers? (8)

7 Host certainly not leggy? (4)

8 River, run (4)

12 New river in Asia designed for old flagship (5,5)

13 Excellent punishment (8)

14 Will writer check schedule that's arisen? (8)

16 See 21

19 Finish wiping bottom after an excess in sticky substance (6)

20 Comeuppance for Theresa May and a Conservative party (4)

21,24,16 6 23 etc to call up among banal and pathetic plays (4,8,8)

Solution see page 277

ACROSS

1 Vegetable served after a special introduction to Alan Sugar backfired (9)

6 Right to withdraw from deal with milk supplier (4)

8 European city home to heart of religious relic (8)

9 Herb wanting space in flower bed (6)

10 Item found in dock? (6)

11 Cooks receiving letter about items on the house? (8)

12 Unpopular Soviet leader visiting a German POW camp ... (6)

15 ... sanctioned over participating in the bombing of Dresden (8)

16 Elegant plot about broadcast (8)

19 Discount English book with standard jacket (6)

21 No points awarded to amateur coming back for old elephant (8)

22 Relish being fashion designer in large house (6)

24 Book deal in trouble (6)

25 Trader supposed to go round royal church (8)

26 Moccasin chosen to cover part of foot (4)

27 Pal drinking shake ordered to get a move on (4,5)

DOWN

1 Enlightened American overcoming battle with drug (5)

2 Hairstyle involving plait twisted around bottom parts of wig (7)

3 Bar set up for merrymaking (5)

4 Boss detailed to catch Irish animal (7)

5 Submit to European rule after university clergyman's in post (9)

6 Options shown here for sailor accepting request by bishop (4,3)

7 Teenager prepared to accept central part of farmer's contract ... (9)

13 ... but destroyed a giant hen (4,5)

14 Ms Garland beaten in top score at the bridge table (5,4)

17 Very large beetroot served with full-flavoured bird (7)

18 A doctor trapped in station went on the rampage (3,4)

20 Upturned vessel containing a Catholic Church deity (7)

22 Fish with rod (5)

23 Clean dirty weapon (5)

Solution see page 277

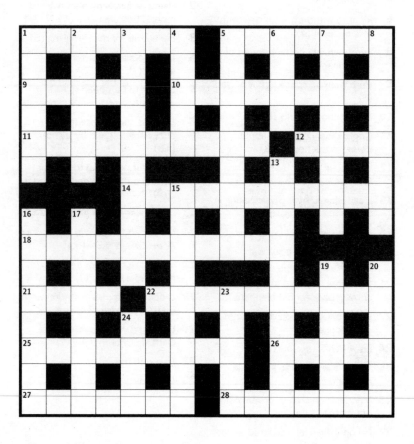

ACROSS

1 Space station with a name (7)

5 Getting a partner rowing? (7)

9 Guardian nursing river country (5)

10 Case of drink (oil of rum) (9)

11 Pleasurable indulgence — sexed up element of Jane Austen work? (10)

12 See 2

14 Linear DIY assistance that might be quickly withdrawn (4,7)

18 Published song by editor on the smaller side (11)

21 Sides removed from metal framework channel (4)

22 Aged female impersonator reverses tide to pat tomcat (3,3,4)

25 Hero cited fanciful four-syllable foot (9)

26 "Drugs kill" bar (5)

27 One who concludes holding company is device to make text unreadable? (7)

28 Model imitation houses set boundaries (7)

DOWN

1 Sweet timid sort welcomes sex (6)

2,12 Discovering it sends homeowner up the wall (6,4)

3 Colourful climber throws tantrums crossing icy Ural peaks (10)

4 Acting penfriend has no measure of dismay (5)

5 Casual piece — watch? (4-5)

6 Provided the central of this sentence (4)

7 United's a member of football division (2,6)

8 First two of irritating Pogues' wayward followers (8)

13 Walked like a confined prisoner in stockinged feet, which prevents self-harm (6,4)

15 Penguin's blueish ruffles breaking up pair? (9)

16 Dish of pork topping and gold hog's back (8)

17 Fit a line to break the involuntary response (8)

19 Times cutting report base (6)

20 Remembered exactly Dicky having stroke (3,3)

23 Book scan reveals money (5)

24 Worthy attempt to use too much (4)

Solution see page 278

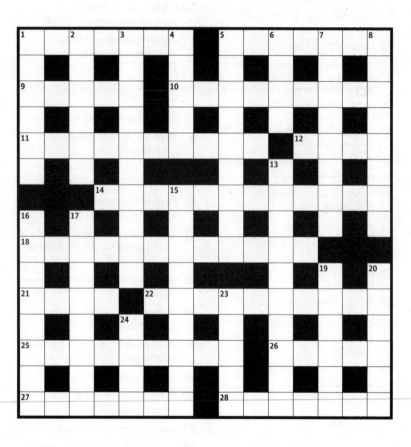

ACROSS

1 Extremely hairy Philistine reaches party in high spirits (5,2)

5 In 26 without, say, a type of hat (4,3)

9 Frenchman with money for second drink (5)

10 Rake one chap used in occupation (9)

11 Some lemon has HNO3 containing carbon instead of nitrogen (6,4)

12 Party without a break (4)

14 Puzzling row about a cowshed (hint: suspect not English) (12)

18 Making holy doctors snort cocaine (12)

21 Broadcast fictions which give substance to soaps? (4)

22 My crime? Sat around, being crooked (10)

25 Journo backed definition that's undignified (9)

26 Subject of story told by Georgia (5)

27 Problem getting old Times supplement? (7)

28 Go wrong injecting soft enzyme (7)

DOWN

1 "Hello, sailor" is appropriate, when moving (6)

2 Devout former judge and governor (6)

3 Copies potential partners, keeping mostly upbeat? (10)

4 President leading a merry dance? (5)

5 "Biopic strewn with lust, not love" (Advertiser) (9)

6 Thin artist reluctantly eating starters (4)

7 Hook holding one black French dressing gown (8)

8 Spared once seduced, when short of time (8)

13 City about right latitude for common sort of golf tournament (6,4)

15 Standard measures for ale? That's right (9)

16 Stops only child Penny filling in part of crossword (8)

17 Stop for a time in Bury, meeting male having sex (8)

19 Topless match, with players from one side in shades (6)

20 Blind test? (6)

23 In power, May's tense (5)

24 Old man, twice party leader (4)

Solution see page 278

Set by Paul

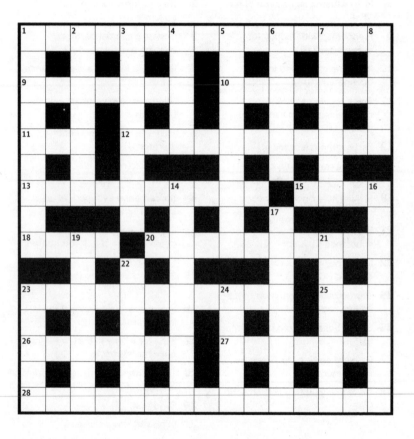

ACROSS

1 Promotion offering sex in the open air? (6,9)

9 Puzzle only negative? (7)

10 Powerful beast, south-west Indian stream it's suggested? (7)

11 Lighter materials under packages (3)

12 Genius doctor hugged by sweetie (5,6)

13 Bewildering debts cut, or stopped (10)

15 Drifter accommodated by millionaires? No way! (4)

18 Hitch lacking success after film score (4)

20 Play about Genesis (10)

23 Live by chance (2,2,7)

25 See 8

26 Cuddle sweetheart 1002? (7)

27 City assuming footballer's first to join club, perhaps? (7)

28 John Lennon has one song left before dying (7,8)

DOWN

1 Writer is character in Yorkshire market town (9)

2 Hand up the pole (7)

3 Imagined America in attack showing no leadership (8)

4 A celebrity finally reaching the top, Jamaican perhaps? (5)

5 Extraordinary way gay Hitler minced (5,4)

6 Supercharged time for swimmer (6)

7 Nicking case of liqueurs, pleb in raincoat (7)

8,25 Technologically advanced spring on base of hinge in prison (5-3)

14 Those baked on the plains of Manitoba? Temperature most disturbing (9)

16 Cracking whip lower down initially fun (9)

17 Bum note concealed by West Midlands boomer (4,4)

19 Originally cost flexible, one going up (7)

21 One overcoming queen, an Islamic republican (7)

22 Inferior company accepting lots (6)

23 Patch around surface of nose ring (5)

24 Host ends in house from chronic fatigue syndrome (5)

Solution see page 278

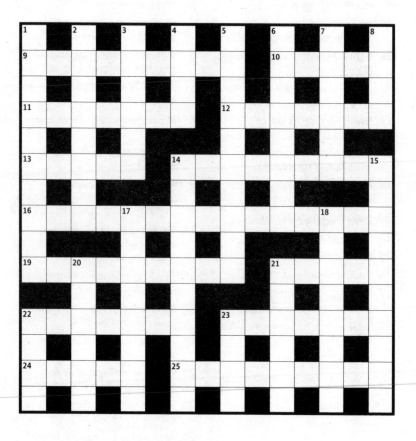

ACROSS

9 Cryptically, how she runs home (9)

10 Bare land here (5)

11 Free to go through again, retaining key (7)

12 Girl joining society left in first-class mess (7)

13 Tip: fill the gaps between 7 (5)

14 Drool goes everywhere — he takes it on the chin (4,5)

16 Users get authors to change one of their sources (6,9)

19 Yen increased, provided one invested and got smarter? (9)

21 He dresses mother and child (5)

22 Turner cherished small silver dish (7)

23 Did nurse prepare Mark for weariness? (7)

24 Fine chimney in Glasgow backs on to court (5)

25 Pass priest eating Northern Irish food (9)

DOWN

1 Insurance for Lib Dems? (5,5)

2 Mike secretly tackling the Italian racket in construction (8)

3 Bond writer comes into a little money (6)

4 Lost boring game? That's old hat (4)

5 Contest what bad pupils are told to do? (4-2-4)

6 Is Lincoln entirely standing up queen? (8)

7 Reliable types initially keen to crack emerging economies (6)

8 Part of church, perhaps eastern section (4)

14 Sack actor, high with cocaine, opening at the Abbey? (6,4)

15 Bitterness to do with feeling one's ignored (10)

17 What pushy drivers do to gain entrance to estate (8)

18 Local chairman's heading off (8)

20 It crushes steel forged under pressure (6)

21 Hawk carries this weapon (6)

22 Story about male constituent of 21 (4)

23 Run off some cloth from old mill town on leaving (4)

Solution see page 279

92 Set by Vlad

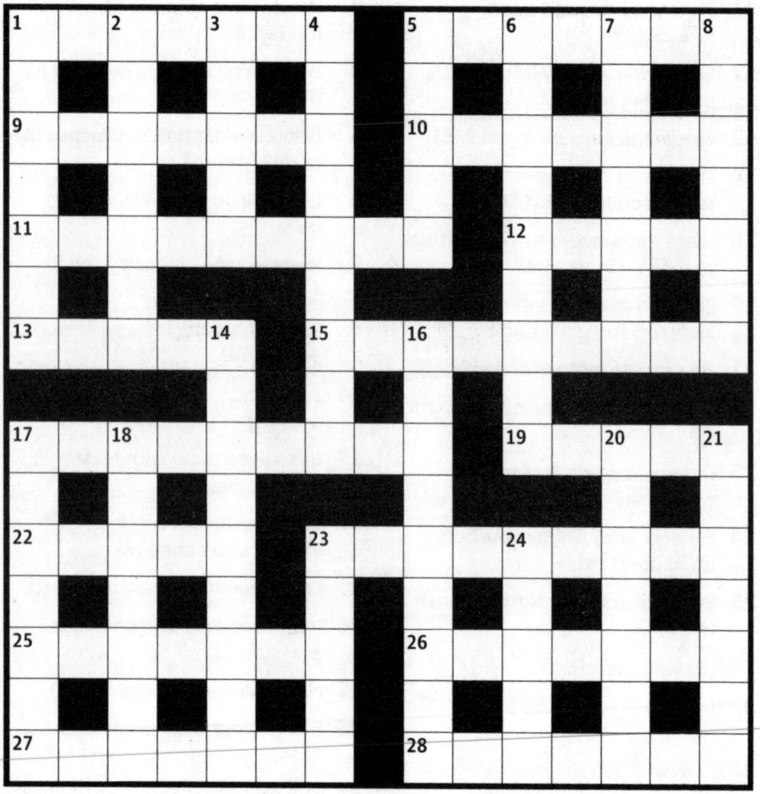

ACROSS

1 Job description (7)

5 Fish's journey across rough water (4,3)

9 Sweet face about to fall (7)

10 Do like it when current partner's around (7)

11 Where old conservationist was keeping department ignorant (2,3,4)

12 Why I 'ad to return (5)

13 Chap my boss made fun of (5)

15 Surveyed scans A&E produced over 5d (9)

17 Raises environment finally with Green politician (4,5)

19 Readily accept return of an immature creature (3,2)

22 Doctor's on to sickness in French port (5)

23 Minder — Terry initially absent from start of story (9)

25 Provided car with wing missing — dodgy in the extreme (7)

26 Game Boy's a throwback (7)

27 A scolded bishop ignored bubbly (7)

28 Opening with work in disorder (7)

DOWN

1 Springer regularly does it in a sticky situation (7)

2 In college upset your old man (7)

3 Scary country, Spain after revolution (5)

4 Entertainer? Time stripper got topless! (3,6)

5 Well in credit, Henry invested (5)

6,7 Alarmed half of Tory ladies, I fancy, including these? (5,4,7)

8 Argued case for penny on petrol, sort of (7)

14 His doesn't work — it's bent (9)

16 Can one settle comfortably outside city? (9)

17 Island's very good on the surface — stick around! (7)

18 Conservative strongly backing demand (4,3)

20 Not requiring payment for singer (3,4)

21 Priest and sweetheart like sexy underwear in church office (7)

23 Speaking with sense is commended (5)

24 System meant to hold up West Country tourist (5)

Solution see page 279

93 Set by Vulcan

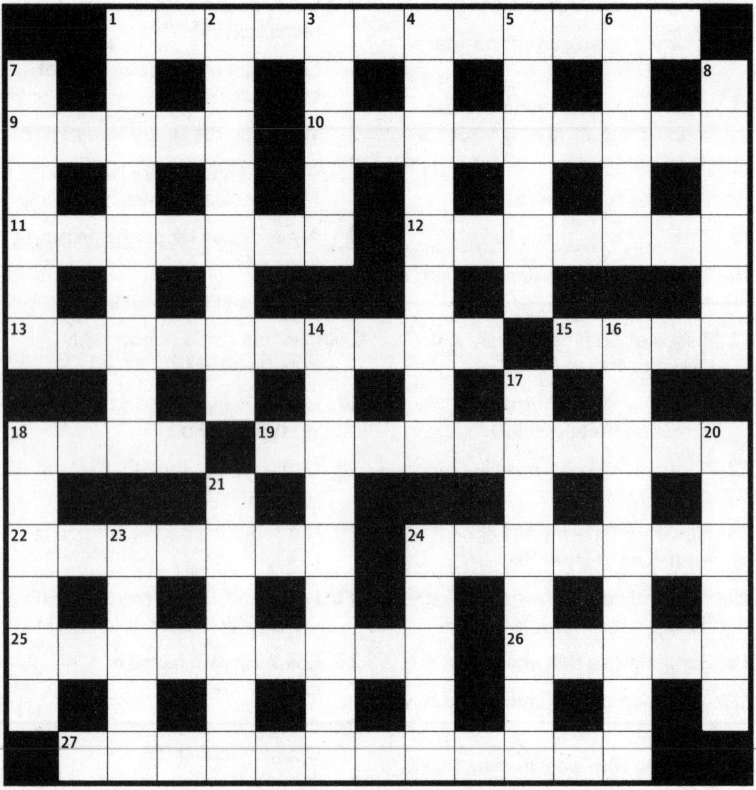

ACROSS

1 Very exciting case in court, absolutely full (6–6)

9 Sky thus clearer, as university sportsman runs (5)

10 Australian who believes in evolution? (9)

11 One showing appreciation of tongue (7)

12 Pen — only touched one end? (4-3)

13 Where one was punished, until completely motionless (5-5)

15 Change feet over (4)

18 Witches can't start cooker (4)

19 Setting out virtues of joining euro? (10)

22 The arts of growing lab specimen? (7)

24 Prime us acting for those standing in the middle (7)

25 No more jokes after this, said to be the longest? (4,5)

26 Half hope to take advantage of building (5)

27 Need contract revised but not watered down (12)

DOWN

1 Distinctly superior cave about to be transformed (1,3,5)

2 Go and fish below the old road (8)

3 Give instructions for tidiness (5)

4 Range of investments: poor lot, if badly managed (9)

5 Cold countryside at first and not flat (6)

6 Proclamation wrongly cited (5)

7 Counter on which one may tell one's beads? (6)

8 Quickly buy pans suggested (4,2)

14 Refund from the Revenue? (3,6)

16 Suddenly turn to make a collection (4-5)

17 Picture that striker quickly takes (8)

18 Secret business, turning up at sect (6)

20 Fuel kept without pressure seal (6)

21 Sort of school for everyone? Yes and no (6)

23 Rope, look, tethering donkey (5)

24 Escort drug dealer for execution (5)

Solution see page 279

ACROSS

5 Work hard on a new catchphrase (6)

6 Composition for soprano working with Australian tenor and alto (6)

9 Heartless publisher to get rid of French author (6)

10 Oscar trophy found in tin by actor's third tenant (8)

11 Buffet always includes dairy product (4)

12 Unpleasant character found by retired cops merrymaking in empty clink (6,4)

13 Beaten miner agreed with the police (11)

18 Italian woman cautious about wine (10)

21 Juicy drink (4)

22 Bullets containing iron used by tribal leader in hard-fought battle (8)

23 Save soldiers with special signal (6)

24 Pout about extremely expensive hair product (6)

25 Crafty poet married Iris (6)

DOWN

1 Mate taking money into shelter (8)

2 Pole in charge of sticky stuff (6)

3 Real centre of democracy on Greek island (8)

4 Minor embracing exercise is not in good shape (6)

5 Dish found in scenery outside Globe (6)

7 Setter leaving injured American's treatment for bruises (6)

8 Old German revolutionary tucked into dish of fruit (11)

14 Philosopher stops working to get hold of Socrates' second book (8)

15 Difficult universal and timeless tale is deceptive (8)

16 Ski lodge in Switzerland rented out after the beginning of April (6)

17 Problems in editions? (6)

19 Cloth covering unacceptable stew (6)

20 Flipping badger eating root of brassica plant (6)

Solution see page 280

ACROSS

1 Tides swirling round end of bus stop (6)

4,23 Try to get friend into new art and old Marian hymn music (6,5)

9 Couple stealing gold from home helper (4)

10 Money given to fourth in line, say, for property (4,6)

11 Round clubs for the old man (6)

12 Let down by legal document about apartment (8)

13 Cruel and pointed remark by one born in late March? (9)

15 Accommodation for archaeologists? (4)

16 Part of the Koran found in ancient city in Saudi Arabia (4)

17 One travelling out to north Germany (9)

21 Itinerant magician's prop turned King Edward into Queen Elizabeth! (8)

22 Drink, one way and another, leads to disturbance (6)

24 Craftsman means to groom his boy (10)

25 Ass featured in ancient witchcraft (4)

26 River bird may be a record holder (6)

27 Soldiers leaving train for another kind of transport (6)

DOWN

1 Excitement about Switzerland's old silver coin (7)

2 Cancel subscription to protect creditor (5)

3 Streetwise leader's entreaty to graffiti artist? (7)

5 Upper-class chap snorting drugs to get things going (3,3)

6 Taliban to become an army unit (9)

7 Pre-rest, naughty child moves unsteadily (7)

8 Vehicles, one after another, carrying assistance, turned up to support a major medical emergency (7,6)

14 Damaged car banned in social event (4,5)

16 Set up celebrity with young man from the fifties (7)

18 Sergeant abroad missing English rum (7)

19 European charged outside America is difficult to catch (7)

20 Atrocity committed on a field of battle? (6)

23 See 4

Solution see page 280

Set by Pasquale

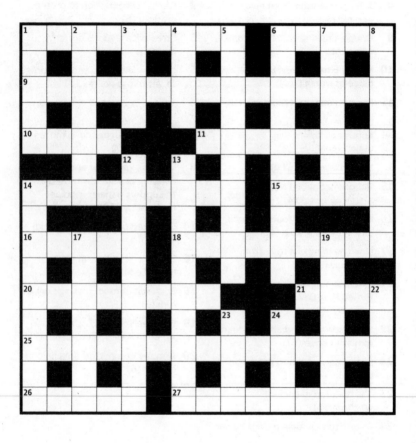

ACROSS

1 Dramatist's second work — this classical reading son ignored (9)

6 Shift gear initially, entering seaside resort (5)

9 Recalculate so as to change part of business contract (9,6)

10 Man of Enterprise in Scottish place of worship (4)

11 In Paris I may meet Sam who sells valuable items? (8)

14 Raft we all abandoned — unnavigable part of river? (9)

15 Party food — for Americans (5)

16 Raucous sound of bird (5)

18 Something unsightly hiding pretty trees (9)

20 Classical composer, while avoiding extremes, has place for rock (8)

21 Back religious believer almost to the end (4)

25 Italian footballer and friend entertaining Tranmere team in a contentious manner (15)

26 Ropy stuff in clues is allowed, putting a lot off (5)

27 The fellow designated to engage one showed indecision (9)

DOWN

1 Catch son having kiss and cuddle (5)

2 American hoarder of Sinatra, F and chums, so to speak? (4,3)

3 Airport in a bad way — work abandoned after upset (4)

4 Naval officer and author having destiny on island (4)

5 Avant garde type from south-east county, mostly associated with top people (10)

6 Audible encouragement to William in communication of love? (6,4)

7 Mound of food's ending with drink? Nothing turned up (7)

8 Curses river's decrepit transport (9)

12 Like some music that gives backing to R Charles, possibly (10)

13 University zone, one sealed off very briefly (gosh!) after pub room ceremony (3,7)

14 Charge forefathers try out in hostile moves (3,9)

17 Nymphs, any number in bras and panties? (7)

19 One of a number of children sequentially evident in Alcott tale (7)

22 Female in woods is crazy, showing no feelings for male (5)

23 Navy limited by unserviceable vessels (4)

24 Suggestion inadequate, first to last (4)

Solution see page 280

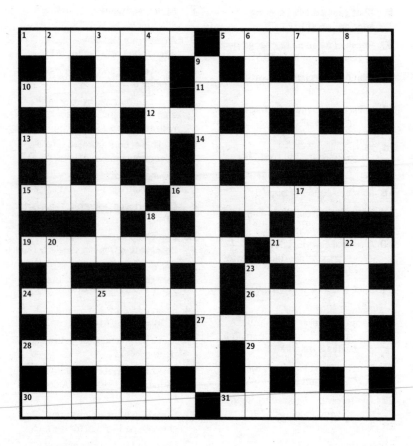

ACROSS

1,29 Got near the solution to this, but not overly impressive (2,5,6)

5 Seductresses help removing our uniform — twice (7)

10 Engaged Asian picked up at party (4,2)

11 Prints articles initially in the City (8)

12 Priest's among non-believers (3)

13 Invest in road building (6)

14,30 New guy starts to renegotiate cheap fee for each writer (8,7)

15 Bungling Italy on three points (5)

16 Choice woman's finally made to leave? Hear it's fallacious (9)

19 Close to broke in most of country — no alternative to Tory policy? (9)

21 Tea next to instant coffee (5)

24 One piece of writing in leaflet is less convincing (8)

26 Doris's entertaining fellow when things go wrong (3-3)

27 Matter of disrespect (3)

28 Hearts lost twice — that coach's messed up direction to players (8)

29 See 1

30 See 14

31 Son went on Big Dipper in these? (7)

DOWN

2 Mike's a different bloke after love letter (7)

3 Course favourite gets special welcome (3,6)

4 Join in with degree course, initially (6)

6 Nancy's a fool getting man to strip (8)

7 Bluff a national treasure? (5)

8 Tap on counter — a quarter admitted it's annoying (7)

9 Order given to ignore boner under newspaper — a dreadful rule! (5,2,6)

17 'E's upset about current criticism (one of a generation that's easily offended) (9)

18 Water right for fellow in one ship (8)

20 Open jar at lunch (7)

22 Carrying drugs, must stop boat (5,2)

23 Energy drink a bit special is inside talk (6)

25 Historian set out for Chinese region (5)

Solution see page 281

ACROSS

1 See 23

4 Beautiful perfume and diamonds both reduced (6)

9 Couples playing golf? Female left (4)

10 Converts pounds and euros to cut taxes (10)

11 Warning shouts at the first from Tiger Woods (6)

12 American bar with players — tense meeting at the end (8)

13 Golf? Managed two days with terribly sad old men (9)

15 Pack up trophies in retirement (4)

16 John Daly finally has something to fear (4)

17 Right, take in lead on second shot? (9)

21 Clubs turned on men — is private part for woman? (8)

22 Plant fruit trees here? One for middle of park (6)

24 Ian Poulter upset about an outburst (10)

25 In Baltimore a player makes cut (4)

26 Place to rest? (6)

27 Opposition regularly says "guys": unknown Yankee interrupts (6)

DOWN

1 Lounge and look at sport, turned over to follow golf score (7)

2 Tungsten and lead club (5)

3 Left nets caught up (7)

5 See 19

6 Off tee, Norman gets distance (9)

7 Rest to enter competition to make big bucks (5,2)

8 Rough grassland: side which might go on greens? (5,8)

14 Club close to tee on hole (9)

16 Land ball at the back, stand to welcome American (7)

18 Tiger gutted over short 19 5 round: something on fairway? (7)

19,5 Rory McIlroy nearly up a shot — like either of two that make green? (7,6)

20 American player, Tom, to progress smoothly (6)

23,1across It spices up Ryder Cup: row turns nasty (5,6)

Solution see page 281

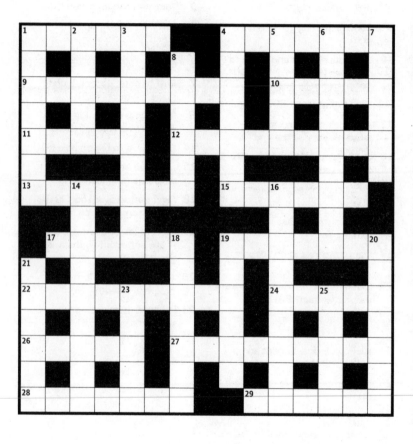

ACROSS

1 Musician's book is lacking support (6)

4 Advanced because fighting Germany (7)

9 Data not in for Red Arrows display? (9)

10 Long-distance traveller needs to reach Everest's base (5)

11 One's exercise at 50? Get going! (5)

12 Effusive, improvised C sharp setting for groom's vow rejected (9)

13 Barperson who has a sip (about a pint) (7)

15 Caught in lie about old advocate's outfit (6)

17 Speaker's position, bottom of heap — shame (6)

19 Weed brings illness and bereavement (7)

22 Lacking competition, large organisation sat after work (9)

24 Submit pill when temperature's taken (5)

26 Feature of fencing's noisy collapse (5)

27 Turn the screw left not right ultimately, to relax? (7,2)

28 Play ten rounds as punishment (7)

29 Who might pierce inner ear, being vexed about Queen and Church (6)

DOWN

1 Fact: if swimming round lake, that's trouble (7)

2 Short cut round T-bar (5)

3 Castrati failed to comprehend Latin composer (9)

4 Sweet, affectionate article on collection of books (7)

5 Meeting different sorts of people (5)

6 Jocular, mad, illogical centre for protected species (9)

7 To get unengaged, the chap had to take Kitty back (6)

8 Spanish artist admits resistance against reverse driving aid (6)

14 Sales publicity for poet? (9)

16 Who thinks Rocky too tragic? (9)

18 Avoid stage production broadcast: it might infringe the rules (7)

19 Rogue commanded galleons originally (3,3)

20 Second one to cry "Besom"? (7)

21 Pound no good — raise (4,2)

23 Feature of flower power: raised behind (5)

25 Sands (new for start of athletics) settle (5)

Solution see page 281

100

Set by Puck

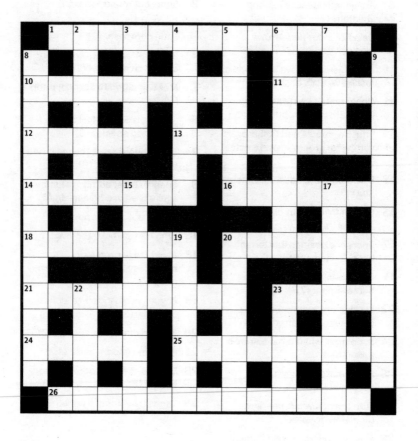

ACROSS

1 Fleet Street's original old man about to do wrong and injure a lawyer (7,6)

10 One reportedly made secure investment choice? (4,5)

11 Type of dressing essential for burn (5)

12 Pressgate? (5)

13 Where rest of ham never returned during wedding party? (9)

14 Mischief-maker follows a game live (7)

16 Sweet bread hot around Luxembourg (7)

18 Related couple dance round in church (7)

20 Meets regularly in wooded valley estate (7)

21 Inconvenience of one new wee chair? (9)

23 Good porridge rejected, if US version (5)

24 One dressed in black: flipping stoned mourner? (5)

25 Lobby against sporting blue ties (9)

26 Dog, having cocked up leg in street, keeps quiet (7,6)

DOWN

2 Infecting one's leg with iodine — and, sadly, no GP around (9)

3 Famous day school? On the contrary (5)

4 Arms raised and leg bent to get comfy? (7)

5 Current Hair cast member (7)

6 Give fake news to schoolgirl, say? (9)

7 Sorry, I can't help you up on horse first (5)

8 Wife, not daughter, has arranged a discount, going round sales with lowered prices (5,8)

9 Illness caused by bug — one given various names by the French (6,7)

15 A batter collecting runs, cricketer Warner (5,4)

17 Dog bitten by dog and bone gets fatigue (9)

19 Goes round topless, then matures (7)

20 Clothing medic top and bottom in scrubs? (7)

22 Top part of grid in empty column (5)

23 Corny stuff in act Sir Galahad served up (5)

Solution see page 282

101

Set by Chifonie

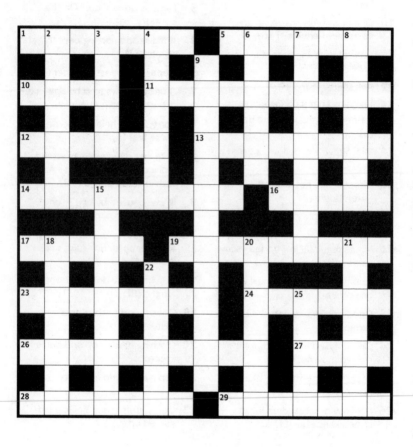

ACROSS

1 Holds sailor's balls (7)

5 Girl embraces joiner in porch (7)

10 Husband has time for divinity (4)

11 Relaxing preparation frees communications, 19 (3–7)

12 Honest conduct (6)

13 See patient's wallet (8)

14 Remains an outside agent for museum (9)

16 Wade across outlying island's inlet (5)

17 Angry about Tory result (5)

19 Primarily at sea? (2,3,4)

23 Fret about exam for puritan (8)

24 Airline has lots of clubs (6)

26 Killjoy has loot left (10)

27 Small boat found in the Channel (4)

28 Familiars have demons kidnapping redhead (7)

29 A model cares for chaperones (7)

DOWN

2 Fungus moved by wind? It is! (7)

3 Love to rebuke and pontificate (5)

4 City with old railway company first linked to Circle line (7)

6 Birds go initially into rustling trees (6)

7 A rich man's moved by anti-government argument (9)

8 Lady's maid found showing off in the kitchen (7)

9 Sacred belief in control over motor race (13)

15 Soldier eats fish spread (9)

18 Policeman seizes Hungarian leader's weapon (7)

20 Environment Tabitha created (7)

21 Passed by ruin on ridge (7)

22 Partisan located outside Indian capital (6)

25 Anita Stewart shows discrimination (5)

Solution see page 282

ACROSS

9 Roman coins and dinosaur Einstein excavated (5)

10 Professionally, I say pinch boil to get better (9)

11 They obstruct retired NHS doctor, wasting time (9)

12 Stories are cliched from beginning to end (5)

13 Protected and paid to be free of bugs within? (7)

15 Good girl travels with male traveller (7)

17 Catholic soon to be 23 (5)

18 I would take back pawn with pawn ... (3)

20 ... to develop rook first, then knight, following training (5)

22 Show best speed, perhaps? (3,4)

25 Contributes Qaos and Tramp's puzzles (7)

26 Conservative member gets to rise (5)

27 Aardvarks are very hard to confine in storage building (5-4)

30 Paper's reporters (9)

31 23, 100, 50, er ... 1,000? (5)

DOWN

1 It's held by club at Hull City (4)

2 Soul sister's founding father (8)

3 Partner (or partners) provided within (4)

4 Piddles all over the place — take in note, it's impressive! (8)

5 Henry's bouquet wrapped up small flower (6)

6 You can get hold of a piece with this (6,4)

7 Novelist whose work is a bit of a grind? (6)

8 Workers' tirades: "Right To Strike" (4)

13 Fancy topic: Embroidery Stitch (5)

14 Agree to massage back after jog in Kent (10)

16 IMHO, snakes regularly become religious figures (5)

19 Head of convent earlier was miles away from confusion (8)

21 Old queen admits: "Executed? I'll forgive you" (8)

23 Clergyman most sorry to lose key (6)

24 Local officials, historically, turn up on drugs (6)

26 Heat? It's freezing over — absolute zero! (4)

28 Remove lid from jar to serve wine (4)

29 Benefit of drink? (4)

Solution see page 282

Set by Puck

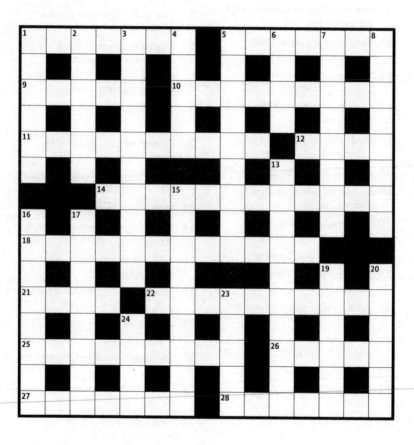

ACROSS

1 Called Island about band member (7)

5 Accumulates trouble below and on high (5,2)

9 Start working group (5)

10 Dismisses backing band twice before show starts (4-5)

11 King or queen beyond rabbit hole? It's hard to say (10)

12 See 6

14 Start of true love? Licks honey, prepared for French kissing (6,6)

18 Query reason for neatness (5,2,5)

21 See 19

22 Air complaint for Mavis (4,6)

25 Wooden home beside main road across northern China (9)

26 Ring doctor about card game (5)

27 Detective showing face around Oxford? (7)

28 Umpteenth rallentando's hidden charm (7)

DOWN

1 Bad jokes about parking in the capital (6)

2 Deny any connection with row about female (6)

3 Car (rattletrap), one that goes on and on (10)

4 Reportedly one that's gone off soft leather (5)

5 Variable length, once absorbed in respectable screw (9)

6,12 Slap fool that's left for Germany (8)

7 Small child gets into wrong Ford in Bulgarian capital (8)

8 Speaks about taking the lead from Yorkshire and Surrey openers (4,4)

13 Painful condition making a horse trot unevenly (4,6)

15 Kill time in US cafe, around about half four (9)

16 Punishment from cross man (8)

17 Refuse to acknowledge detective's right (8)

19,21 Stare at Johnny before kiss (10)

20 Someone having tooth extracted that likely heads for small town in eastern Europe? (6)

23 Birds raised in these eggs (5)

24 Tongue-in-cheek, helpful tips for a small person (4)

Solution see page 283

ACROSS

9 Reason one is entertained by beer-swilling vermin? (9)

10 Singer of serenade, Lennon (5)

11 Extremity of foot on swine? (7)

12 See 16

13 Attractive person shaved for public display (4)

14 Sleeping around, breed regularly like rabbits? (3-7)

16,12 Possible shocker, business news (7,7)

17 Reason Trump needs bottom wiped, incompetent US politician (7)

19 Phrase, fast one working (10)

22 Brandy, stuff knocked back (4)

24 Very many in dish with 24 blackbirds, say? Then bird finally flew (7)

25 Those in the pit not entirely fearful about God (7)

26 Thread referring to the night before (5)

27,2 Noble Swedish retailer, tucking into terribly poor stew, right to curse privately? (5,4,1,7)

DOWN

1 The Spanish worm has filled comrades' shoes (7,8)

2 See 27

3 Training target absurd (5)

4 Most dangerous horse finally caught by girl in Kentucky Derby, perhaps? (8)

5 God rises over local angel (6)

6 Clue about a drink describing strong little tipple (4,1,4)

7 Body removed from grave? Little sign (6)

8 I've got your communication, as by some modem or nanotechnology? (7,8)

15 Figure gathering spotted coats (9)

17 Why the limp position? (5,3)

18 Tiny boy penning a song for a drink (3,5)

20 Cut off old thumb (6)

21 Pious type caging a wicked god, the brute (6)

23 Stylish sting (5)

Solution see page 283

Set by Tramp

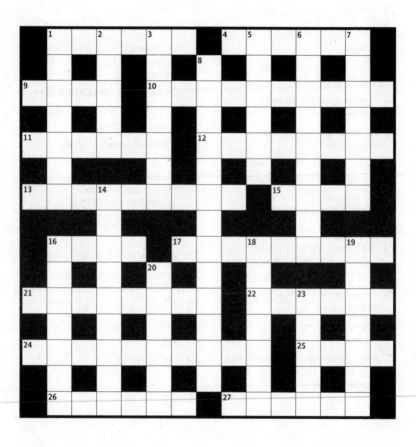

ACROSS

1 Half of really friendly city (6)

4 Shoot right rabbit on fencing (6)

9 In which soldiers may drop bombs (4)

10 More than one quashing — mental nuns wrestling (10)

11 See 16

12 Picture headless cartoon character in short episode (8)

13 Home time — one shot to capture route (9)

15 Director having sex, second pair of smalls discarded (4)

16,11 Controlling back of Wallace and Gromit in animation (10)

17 Fast runner to show off brand (6,3)

21 Vegetable with potassium? Cooks boil hard leaves off end (8)

22 Primarily Shaun the Sheep dead drunk (6)

24 Late talks for groups of clergymen (10)

25 Took home wheels for cheese (4)

26 Stops to collect Oscar with awards (6)

27 See 20

DOWN

1 Tramp turning over telly, catching A Grand Day Out (7)

2 North American native that is wrong to be upset (5)

3 Cock-up by one in animated series? (7)

5 Nick Park (4,2)

6 Demands too much with public cuts (9)

7 Great film (7)

8 Wrong trousers cut below hip (13)

14 Due to land, terribly bumpy (9)

16 Money to tie up, fell over time (7)

18 On models, section in middle sticks out (7)

19 Expert presenter of art film, that's clear (7)

20,27 Fine to take off A Close Shave (6,6)

23 Fluid piece from René Magritte (5)

Solution see page 283

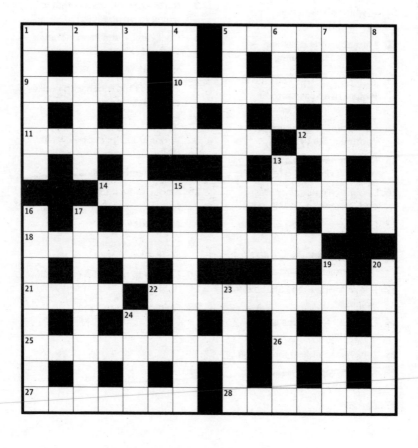

ACROSS

1,18 Duplicitous as in political sphere, also phoniest allies, pair struggling to maintain conceit, primarily? (7,12)

5 See 21

9 Somewhere in Asia, hotel's neighbour? (5)

10 Sadly, the traditions of US apartments? (3,6)

11 Where Jack accommodated divine liturgy easily, initially (10)

12 See 24

14 One performing delicate work drops into flower (5,7)

18 See 1

21,5 Wearing tie, figure carrying small black jumper (4,7)

22 Man after hit story that's hot (10)

25 Save some nice old works (9)

26 Not exactly a spell (5)

27 Stalk headless monster in bar (7)

28 Bird for Trump? (7)

DOWN

1 Superior numbers ultimately high, one senses? (6)

2 Suffer demise, nation lacking leadership getting comeuppance (6)

3 Where beer may be found to contain copper? Wrong (10)

4 See 6

5 Last two standing in a line wearing boxers? (9)

6,4 Chelsea so poor, Oxford ties? (9)

7 Closed one end up high (8)

8 Soft bowing (8)

13 Pictures I almost deleted, dead say (10)

15 Compound where I'm being carried round on large animal (4,5)

16 Find endless fruit covering lip (6,2)

17 Save bags to have everything you need when power's lost (8)

19 No more time after half of air gone (2,4)

20 Large hole where bottom caught, with fundament in fact squeezed up (6)

23 Toll cut, tax at first went down (5)

24,12 Creator claims to witness decay (2,2,4)

Solution see page 284

107

Set by Arachne

ACROSS

1 Exuberance of black cat (6)

4 Starts to open wine after top award (6)

9 I retired, nursing left eye (4)

10 Arachne engulfed by a campfire, accidentally as it first seems (5,5)

11 British family on island initially imprisoned for skimpy clothing (6)

12 Seeing quite boring people rowing (8)

13 Magic words to stir Tory sheep (3,6)

15 Fool around with unknown Lilliputian (4)

16 Voicing full agreement (4)

17 Alcoholic drink is truly an evil (5,4)

21 Act honourably and skin fruit for Spooner (4,4)

22 Puts spikes behind back of Co-op (6)

24 Playing percussion very fast (10)

25 Lie about money being short (4)

26 Fur coat stolen from Merc store (6)

27 Sentimental drunk wearing Y-fronts inside out and back to front (6)

DOWN

1 Recurrent Gibraltar issue escalating greatly (3,4)

2 Aunt Georgia oddly lacking internal organs (5)

3 Fancy a hundred and thirty days on frozen water? (7)

5 Gentleman enquiring about house paint (6)

6 Custom of not returning to collect bones over time (9)

7 Massive wife, four fifths of a ton (7)

8 Frank tore after dog in DC (6,7)

14 Thick-skinned beast, Mr Hyde on rampage after cover-up (9)

16 Foul pole vault leaving Virginia seething (7)

18 Drinker finally ejected from hot and humid local (7)

19 Kiddies regularly team up, in theory (7)

20 Grandma's tent out of bounds for Arctic explorer (6)

23 Places book of vacuous theatrical anecdotes under "A" (5)

Solution see page 284

108

Set by Philistine

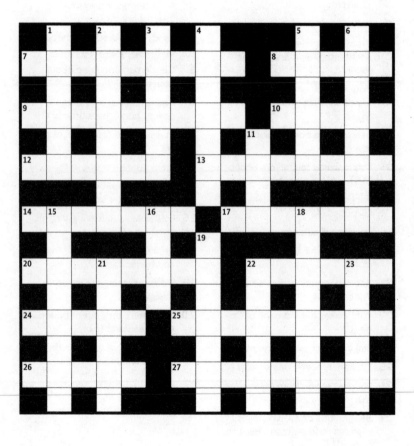

ACROSS

7 Help turned into helping waves (9)

8 Channel something heard well (5)

9 A moonlit romance ultimately makes one thus (9)

10 Declared 48 hours before D-day, what makes privates presentable (5)

12 Going nowhere in commercial break (6)

13 Those against accepting defeat are in the soup (8)

14 Some Laurel and Hardy finally in a fable that's been rewritten (3,4)

17 Decide about a city in the US (7)

20 The next sound as well is a bird (8)

22 Small dog locker with doubled top (6)

24 Start off continent expedition (5)

25 What covers essay by learner is found (9)

26 Flinch from overflow in cesspit (5)

27 Had search party status evaluated externally (9)

DOWN

1 Cultivated member ate out (6)

2 Poor hearing, when one is in the wind (8)

3 All-out extremely tight sumo wrestling (6)

4 Leaves to set up taxi firm (7)

5 Then compete and start to turn red (6)

6 Fiendish foxtrot gives way to tango from within (8)

11 See 16

15 A dreamer with no name is fragrant (8)

16,11 Fancy diet not a cure (8)

18 Credit slip uncovered: don't say a word — it's sensitive (8)

19 Sun now, then rain (7)

21 18 not 51, may be vulgar (6)

22 Harsh lectures to the audience (6)

23 Evenly and softly to begin with, that's right: not so hard (6)

Solution see page 284

109

Set by Vulcan

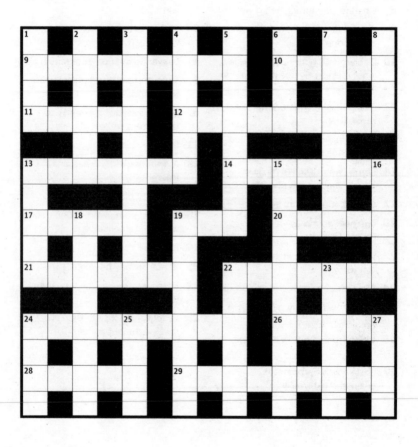

ACROSS

9 The first victim? (5,4)

10 Left in hollow to give birth (5)

11 Men in game who are easily manipulated (5)

12 One short of a majority? (9)

13 Not entirely biased? (7)

14 Taking off from sound in this direction (7)

17 Arab in small car (5)

19 In a team he doesn't pull his weight (3)

20 Open new container of pasta (5)

21 Walk ungainly past front of truck for garbage (7)

22 Horny Scottish supporter (7)

24 Limit on search for food assumed by soldiers (6,3)

26 Dread slithering snake (5)

28 Change dress for hours of work (5)

29 Be unsteady, vital lace coming undone (9)

DOWN

1 Insect lived quietly (4)

2 Farmer, good man in an argument (6)

3 Like some ads to be withheld for security (10)

4 Briefly ask advice of diplomat (6)

5 Does it store things taken off your hands? (8)

6 I study religious figure (4)

7 African with some spice wrapped in sugar? (8)

8 Girl cuts end off trousers (4)

13 Assume one opens the letters (5)

15 Relevant program on TV about Blair regularly skipped (10)

16 Pick up article in valley (5)

18 Brave being involved in a fraud (8)

19 Forcing to break ice cover (8)

22 Clear case? (6)

23 Torture alternative: to bargain (6)

24 Commotion, following American warship (4)

25 Old German received at hospital (4)

27 Bank's not entirely free finance (4)

Solution see page 285

ACROSS

1 Nurse to show soldiers tablet to arouse (8)

5 In retirement, some staff offering to go away (3,3)

9 Girl in group to follow one trained to lead (5,3)

10 Disheartened one in mixed school called for attention (6)

12 Sweep in the morning, empty bags (5)

13 Timber 24? (3-2-4)

14 Brainless act breaking bit of wind (4,8)

18 Lying bums hide beneath their disguise (5,7)

21 Indian being place with hot produce (5,4)

23 6 oddly died on film (5)

24 Boxer twice making excuses for failure (6)

25 Strike pay condition making it hard to walk? (4,4)

26 Attempts papers (6)

27 PC getting off cocaine drunk beers in unknown numbers (8)

DOWN

1 Take on English date (6)

2 Mystery Machine's case, again leader lost Shaggy? (6)

3 Serious Daphne essentially missing Scooby-Doo? (5,4)

4 Meddling kids initially snoop, eh? Most plausible (6-6)

6 Rear characters in Scooby-Doo following one that likes to eat (5)

7 Private 11? (3-2-3)

8 Ally of Freddie regularly dropped charge (8)

11 Firm left recent meeting in a way that's subsidiary (12)

15 Terrible bore, Velma can be detached (9)

16 Bad leg not visible during play (8)

17 They could be vacant females taking debauched one inside? (8)

19 Horrid Scrappy-Doo is taking a turn (6)

20 Top layer runs into bed with old lover (6)

22 Terrifying Shaggy (5)

Solution see page 285

ACROSS

5 Red ring, one covered by pole (6)

6 Little one in big boxes close to dustbin (6)

9 Take on a problem in extremes of solitude (6)

10 Angels beginning to belch amid much ire, unfortunately (8)

11 Time that flies? (4)

12 Marley had these situations hard to break, miser ultimately involved (10)

13 Someone permanently into his work, good he likes to party (11)

18 High — evidently drunk? (10)

21 Hear red fly (4)

22 Cut food into strips, right in the middle of summer? (8)

23,1,5down Porter's observation after self-diagnosing ringworm? (6,8,6)

24 Flashy fishy? (6)

25 Red setter, line in rust (6)

DOWN

1 See 23

2 Scale a scale, short of the bitter end (6)

3 Outsider in high dudgeon — that's about right (8)

4 Castaway not entirely possessing a great singing voice (6)

5 See 23

7 Sensitive skin of tiger, unpleasant (6)

8 Turner's tipple? (11)

14 7 in 7, everything originally from a European city (8)

15 Circling bloom, see wind (8)

16 As a fiddle is so troublesome initially, one of several steps taken? (6)

17 One on top of an elephant, pig climbing off (6)

19 Thyroid problem — it's in the blood (6)

20 Money for the state (6)

Solution see page 285

Set by Puck

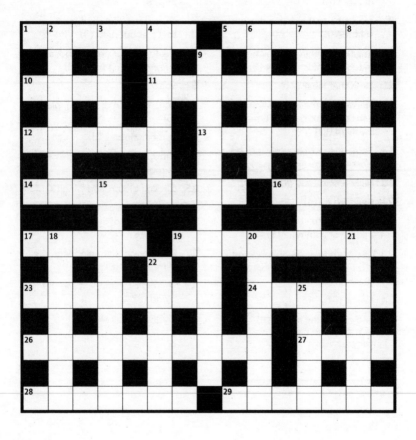

ACROSS

1 System that's used for tax (7)

5 Experienced surgeon operated on European (7)

10,12,24 Police dog that's bound to see evening shower? (4,6,6)

11 Bars supply north-east district (10)

12 See 10

13 Cleavages Simon Peter and Andrew perhaps found pronounced (8)

14 Politician leading English party? False! (7-2)

16,9 Maintain one's composure as warder, say, after row during meal left one a little peeved (4,1,5,5,3)

17 Bill gets sheep to behave badly (3,2)

19 Essential oil obtained from fish in tin? Difficult, if unopened (9)

23 5 12, perhaps (3-5)

24 See 10

26 Bad idea, beginning to interview Trump in warm bathroom (10)

27 See 4

28 Old man? Man possibly unknown in Scottish town (7)

29 Send letter to us that's left out? On the contrary, by the sound of it (5,2)

DOWN

2 Complain bitterly about extremely dear carriage from US (7)

3 An infirm Republican? It's what some believe (5)

4,27 Fish given second light touch to dorsal area (11)

6 Going out with topless degenerate (6)

7 Hedonistic EU prince travelling round Austria (9)

8 Solution has T in place of second P in European port (7)

9 See 16

15 Saint Mungo relocated, with Glasgow initially out of range? (9)

18 Start to climb tree above a volcanic crater (7)

20 Disputed region ready for broadcast on space station (7)

21 Bit of catarrh on child producing wheezing sounds (7)

22 This setter's having quiet drink to follow Vlad's example (6)

25 Superior article at front of book on autonomous computer program (5)

Solution see page 286

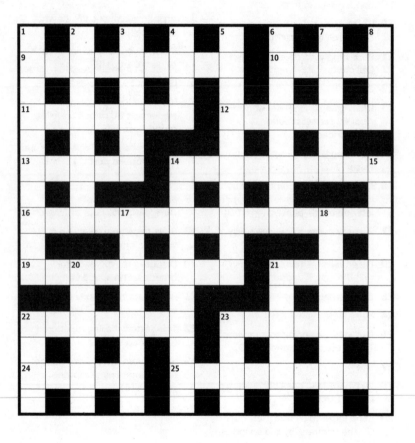

ACROSS

9 Pound nut holding a large stone (9)

10 Popular chestnut fencing timber (5)

11 Fellow member retired during programme (7)

12 Old container brought round before getting pig out (7)

13 Let's stand back to front (5)

14 Obliged school to enrol representative English learners (9)

16 Munch nosh all up, out eating good pub fare (10,5)

19 European Union abandoning work worried complex (9)

21 Tasteful priest delivered clothing (5)

22 Call in agent, getting ruffled? (7)

23 Short work made of some material star collected (7)

24 Rope in Spanish mare at Ascot boxes (5)

25 Wee hit (6,3)

DOWN

1 An American writer describes brief WI music disaster (10)

2 Quietly back complaint in plant (8)

3 Fodder is tossed, then left to mature (6)

4 Finish off incredible eastern story (4)

5 Order people filling in survey to start again (10)

6 Hybrid bulbel the Spanish introduced (8)

7 Suffolk river or its source? (6)

8 A bit like Snowball, short of energy with running (4)

14 Officer carried over short distance with soldier (10)

15 Heated dry nuts, finally parched, desiccated (10)

17 Statesman, say, circulated paper I submitted (8)

18 Emperor shows his dissent, seizing a stick (8)

20,22 Fan mail distributed by branch for 7's 23 across (6,4)

21 Contest opens very tense council (6)

22 See 20

23 Handle staff rises by end of June (4)

Solution see page 286

114

Set by Picaroon

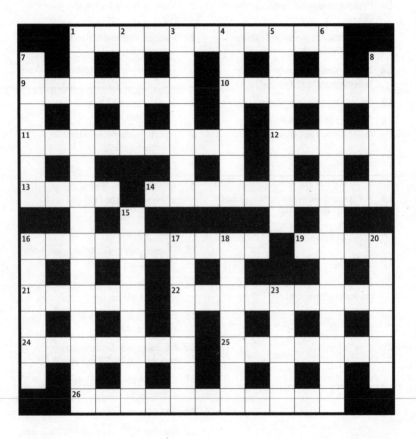

ACROSS

1 Climax that's close, if in posh hot pants (5,6)

9 Maybe Irishman gathering lily in bower (7)

10 Low walls queen knocked over in burial place (7)

11 Overseer of colony's alarmed cry, breaking pager (9)

12 Not a sound president backing Arabian kingdom (5)

13 Land bordering northern cove (4)

14 Make impure drug, cutting what mature people pay (10)

16 Misery, as loot gets left (10)

19 Current ebbing for a change (4)

21 Flowering shrub with flower changing hands (5)

22 Happen to find terrapins at sea (9)

24 Heroin imported by organised crime, a monstrous thing (7)

25 During onset of violence, agreed to be called up (7)

26 Sell fruit outside of Dieppe for everyone (4,2,5)

DOWN

1 A boring dim person interested in being a scientist (15)

2 Suppose it's round and long (5)

3 Love fish, eating best marine creature (7)

4 Perhaps, like Napoleon, avoiding a risk (7)

5 Streams of people arriving like baby Moses? (8)

6 Working man's marched like an emblem of his kind? (6,3,6)

7 What physio may use to kill yak making ascent (3,3)

8 Daughter admitted to knowing online programs (6)

15 Female left male lover carrying a torch (8)

16 Caribbean tree in Cuba is developed (6)

17 Spooner's to install curtain? It's a potential danger (7)

18 It could be Mailer's approach to literature (7)

20 Tense and feeble, like the rural upper classes (6)

23 Number that's square, like four or sixteen (5)

Solution see page 286

115

Set by Brummie

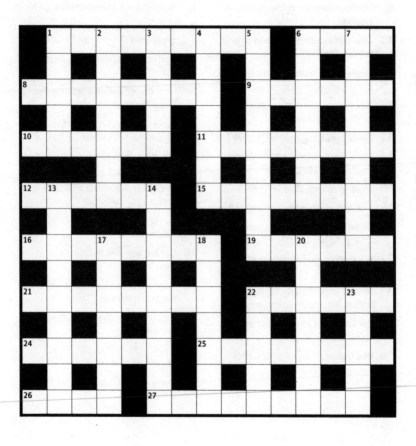

ACROSS

1 Lend money to soldier for a sandwich (9)

6 Biblical ruler has nothing for one's spirit (4)

8 One who would put away other people (8)

9 Reality truly overwhelms sex (6)

10 Stout from May to end of July (6)

11 Dramatic setting relies on rocks (8)

12 Deity's oversize flag (6)

15 Rank insect after fabric (8)

16 Sleeper with composer's visual aid? (8)

19 Dot's fitness class at free prep (6)

21 Tolerate large, upwardly mobile, New York borough (8)

22 In America it's intended to stop partner expecting a series of games (6)

24 Chicken's cry that hurt (6)

25 This exponent of spin may get fired (8)

26 Way to say what Boatman did? (4)

27 Old man, Greek tennis champ, holding supplement (9)

DOWN

1 Cavalryman advanced into ship at sea (5)

2 Ale houses new chain: "Senior Inn Member" (7)

3 It accommodates men in order "to put muscle on the old governor" (5)

4 Breathes over large lens — turned cold? (7)

5 Spy, one right out of abandoned Verdi operas (9)

6 Ecstasy ring expected to stock drug injector? (7)

7 Entire political party rests on English statement (9)

13 Batman of Orpheus carelessly holding up sun god? (9)

14 Dissolute Wally traded in heroin (9)

17 Looked up on the web: "Move both ways, under direction" (7)

18 Was a confessor given fresh air and drink? (7)

20 European leader, in lead, was bloody stoned! (7)

22 Went about reorganising, over deputy's head (5)

23 Mere polluted with yttrium, a hard mineral (5)

Solution see page 287

116

Set by Brummie

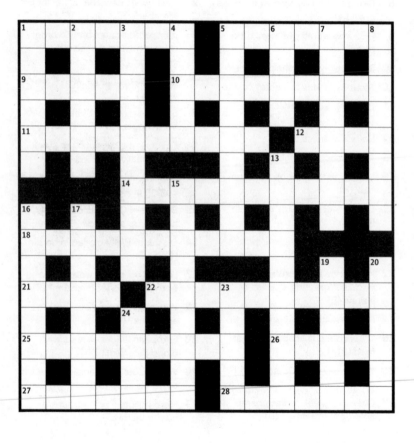

ACROSS

1 Sweet ungulate crossing a river (7)

5 Gangster and ex-chairman thus provided backing internally (7)

9,24 Excited group playing at Fringe (3,2,4)

10 Bitter players engaged in civil disorder (9)

11 Enjoying oneself, when it suits (2,8)

12 A philosopher's works (4)

14 Get shot of Paul? Bottles out! (4,1,6)

18 "Cloth ears" with red mobile (6,5)

21,4 All used up, Tom's a goner (4,5)

22 Want to cut extra evil, vulgar sitcom character (10)

25 Punishing drill, mate — it'll get you nowhere (9)

26 Energy burst Dan's ball? (5)

27 Old instrument gets bird changing key (7)

28 Composer Daniels ends in the middle (7)

DOWN

1 Airline in the money acquires African citadel area (6)

2 Put in another class? Correct (6)

3 Derogatory habit of putting £500 on legal action (6,4)

4 See 21

5 Democrat shot around midpoint of "knoll" procession (9)

6 Leaf used in fencing (4)

7 It produces crude painting, given scope (8)

8 Kiss very upset copper on behind (8)

13 Equal distribution with grand court (10)

15 Very large number getting month off (something charged) (9)

16 Said Buzz, said Mark (8)

17 Pianist ran septet embracing church element (8)

19 Who's a noble Spaniard? A fair character (6)

20 Poet gasping "Retreat!" (6)

23 Intestine that calls for a pause (5)

24 See 9

Solution see page 287

117

Set by Imogen

ACROSS

7 6 pet, a strain to listen to (9)

8 6, a small humble dwelling (5)

9 6 breaks the law, not a person around (9)

10 Sort of sexual underground? (5)

12 Almost nicked, I had to be emotionless (6)

13 English used in a few lines and a few more for comparison (8)

16 Temperature in Holy Land mountain: 6 (7)

19 Firmly fixed wicket into cement base (7)

22 Equipment for police officer, finally and disastrously, closes endless dispute (5,3)

25 6, strong desire to change the ending (6)

27 Record a certain amount but not all 6 (5)

28 6 sounds browner (9)

29 Cheeky husband in 8s 6 (5)

30 Amphibian all but stressed within 6 (9)

DOWN

1 Highly unusual station sign (3,3)

2 Announce holiday cottage available in Andorra for one (8)

3 Served on board, sounding vulgar (6)

4 PC helps reorganise difficult journey (7)

5 Too sensible at first to enter a lift shaft (2,4)

6 An opportunity to learn of this, naturally (6)

11 Beast, decrepit one, losing tail (4)

14 See 15

15,14 6 pounds would get wasted (6)

16 See 17

17,16 6 is back, touring Washington (6)

18 Advantage in battle, if on top of hill (4)

20 Bad year in which to lose an agent (8)

21 Provided for fencing not at first joined together (7)

23 Place to hack into a favourite piece of software (6)

24 Fails to mature topside of beef — roast ruined (6)

25 Book about killer not yet ready (2,4)

26 Pin prick finally punctures needlewoman (6)

Solution see page 287

ACROSS

1 Outer layer that's old, spurning new modern fashion (7)

5 Trade union strike, no adult left out to meddle (7)

9 Relative receives top grade — very well done! (5)

10 West Indian batsman steals silver? I'd go for plum (9)

11 Cry with pain, as scoundrel receives royal warning (6,4)

12 Liberal and Unionist revoke prime minister's block (4)

14 Shift hell's location? (12)

18 Drunk in order to get a measure of annihilation (12)

21 Tried cycling without energy? It's rubbish (4)

22 Ride in a devious way (10)

25 Most remote website regularly finishes 50, 1, 50, 1 (9)

26 Tease American over sweetheart (5)

27 Sign of gas returning? Have to go! (2,5)

28 Bothered to be equipped for winter travel? (7)

DOWN

1 Beginning of boy? Erm … possibly (6)

2 Nothing clear about prophet (6)

3 They work with numbers, sin and cos — to me, it's gibberish (10)

4 Trick with ace (5)

5 Intoxicating Iberian brew, extremely neat (9)

6 Opponents tucking into dry wine (4)

7 Stubbs considered not being entertained (8)

8 Butterfly markings look square close up (8)

13 Soldiers use soap, all lathered up, for changes (10)

15 Deliberately sounding like an American dolphin? (9)

16 Influence and lobby Nobel prize winner (3,5)

17 Nightingale found in Italy (8)

19 Party girl hugs posh boy (6)

20 Kept touring Dorset (6)

23 Score heavily at first, after not getting caught (5)

24 Sluggish car going from 1 to 50? (4)

Solution see page 288

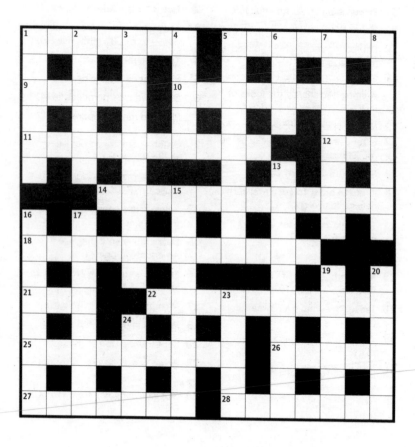

ACROSS

1 Rules over Sweden, then quits (7)

5 Wanting egg, cook troubles servants (7)

9 House 21 (12 read backwards) (5)

10 Subject's alter ego leads plot: the ultimate robbery (9)

11 Styles of penmanship from wearing mittens, by the looks of it (10)

12 National Lottery grips everybody (3)

14 Where they scientifically test Corbyn's speeches? (12)

18 It makes more country sport, helping to protect champion boxers (12)

21 A number of Greek characters retired (3)

22 One in church works outside creating religious music (10)

25 Vice-captain won't worry about Wood not starting (6,3)

26 Noble misses kick-off for Dundee United game (5)

27 Told to raise the spirits, in a way (7)

28 Actor gets fine regarding fake name (7)

DOWN

1 First dogs on Mars? (6)

2 Liquidise drink and pour over naked belly (4,2)

3 Safety barriers on track? (10)

4 Author upset to receive government letter (5)

5 Show fat cats dancing (9)

6 Conservative's pointless lie (4)

7 Pies and mash prepared by weight (8)

8 Initially, sharp back pain, when getting on to girl's telescope (8)

13 Vehicle from space ascending over time takes an age (10)

15 Old plot to capture only Troy was made out of date by Americans (9)

16 Heading for rehabilitation, is one held within Pollsmoor's walls? (8)

17 Expert on IMAX flick left near the end (8)

19 Are two males protecting women's quarters? (6)

20 Infusion served up by shaman, as it pours (6)

23 Snooker mishap, provided no fellow is caught (2-3)

24 Telecom firm acquires another's plant (4)

Solution see page 288

ACROSS

7 Lacking humour, though mostly funny (7)

8 Doctor reveals more than 2 or 3? (7)

9 Keen to go quietly (4)

10 From earliest times, the odd vampire left behind one blood group (9)

12 Not even Bale is Wales' last scorer (5)

13 One writing grand, fine novel — one with cutting edge (8)

15 Regularly looks at TV series (4)

16 Almost hit daughter coming out of one's shower? (5)

17 Some wind from bared US bums (4)

18 See 14

20 Winter sportsmen not right as weather forecasters? (5)

21 Number 4 scores with a boundary (6-3)

22 Team playing in China (4)

24 Tesla faults annoying children? (7)

25 Interval drinks? Event has bottles (7)

DOWN

1 No talking in Hanover Square (4)

2 Steal from Polish characters drunk on flight after vacation (8)

3 Commotion behind the Guardian (6)

4 Side finally leading game — having changed side, won again (8)

5 Joy needs to pull a man (6)

6 Stones' No 1, covered by Prince (4)

11 Politician into initially inept football team? They're getting better (9)

12 Region's flora and fauna in book by Greek character (5)

14,18 Idiot box broadcast ideas for fantastic state of happiness (5,8)

16 Credit Leavers? No question, they're animals to US (8)

17 Wherein one gets stoned — awful dump, I gathered (5,3)

19 Here Norse gods need a second pullover (6)

20 Explicit communication by film group (6)

21,23 Like anteaters and armadillos, say, heading off to back garden? (8)

Solution see page 288

SOLUTIONS

1

2

3

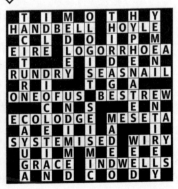

SOLUTIONS

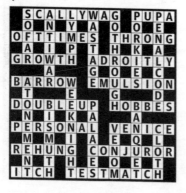

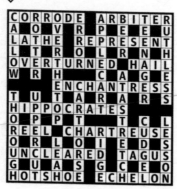

```
C O C K A H O O P     A G E S
L   A   C   F   R   S   A   E
O R D E R   F L U S T E R E D
S   G   O   E   S   R   I   A
E M E R S O N   S H E R B E T
U   S   C   I   T   A   E
P A S S T H E P A R C E L
S   U   H       H   D   A
    B R E A S T F E E D I N G
T   A   B   I   O   R       O
W A L L O O N   U M P T E E N
I   T   A   C   N   A   N   I
S P E A R H E A D   R A V E S
T   R   D   R   E   T   O   E
Y A N K     E A R L Y B I R D
```

```
S   C S   A   A   A G S
P E R T H   S U P E R B R A T
O   O   O   T   E   C O   U
D I S A P P E A R   H O U N D
    S   R   C   D S
H I B A C H I   U S E L E S S
I   A O   S   A       A
T H R U M   K I T   C O W E R
C   M       I   O   I     I
H U B C A P S   D O N A T E S
    A   N   O E       H
B U S E D   W I M B L E D O N
A   S E   E   A   A   R   O
B E E F E A T E R   C R A M P
E   T R O K E   E   A   W E
```

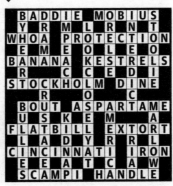

```
B A D D I E   M O B I U S
Y   R   M   L   R   N   T
W H O A   P R O T E C T I O N
E   M   E   O   L   E   O
B A N A N A   K E S T R E L S
R   C   C   E   D   I
S T O C K H O L M   D I N E
    R   O   C
B O U T   A S P A R T A M E
U   S   K   E   M     A
F L A T B I L L   E X T O R T
L   A   D   Y   R   R   L
C I N C I N N A T I   I R O N
E   E   A   T   C   A   W
S C A M P I   H A N D L E
```

SOLUTIONS

10

11

12

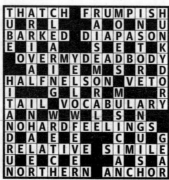

13

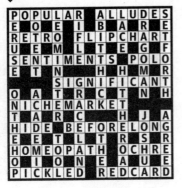

```
P O P U L A R   A L L U D E S
E   O   E   I   B   A   R   E
R E T R O   F L I P C H A R T
U   E   M   L   T   E   G   F
S E N T I M E N T S   P O L O
E   T   N   H   H   M   H   R
      S I G N I F I C A N T
O   A   T   R   C   T   N   H
N I C H E M A R K E T
T   A   R   C   H   J   A
H I D E   B E F O R E L O N G
E   E   T   L   T   R   S   R
H O M E O P A T H   O C H R E
O   I   O   N   E   A   U   E
P I C K L E D   R E D C A R D
```

14

```
  T   P   T       F   A   A
H E N R Y I V   P A R T T W O
  A   O   T       L   B   E
B R A S   B O A R S H E A D
    P   I   N   T   S
  S H E E T   A W A I T I N G
  N   C   S   F       O
W A R T   M O T I F   F A N G
  R   I   A       O   E
T E M P E S T S   B L U N T
  I   T   I   U   R
  A U S T R I A N S   P A D S
  C   T   E   T   A   O
A T W O R S T   Q U I C K L Y
  S   L   S       P   K   L
```

15

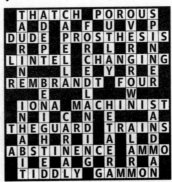

```
  T H A T C H   P O R O U S
  A   D   A   F   U   V   P
D U D E   P R O S T H E S I S
  R   P   E   R   L   R   N
L I N T E L   C H A N G I N G
  N   L   E   Y   R   E
R E M B R A N D T   F O U R
      E       L       W
  I O N A   M A C H I N I S T
  N   I   C   N   E   A
T H E G U A R D   T R A I N S
  A   H   R   I   A   L   D
A B S T I N E N C E   A M M O
  I   E   A   G   R   R   A
  T I D D L Y   G A M M O N
```

SOLUTIONS

 16

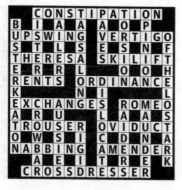

 17

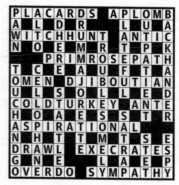

18

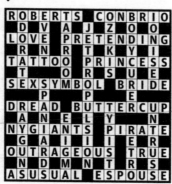

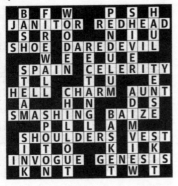

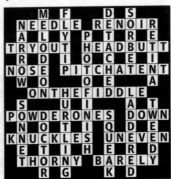

SOLUTIONS

22

```
B E R R I E D   G E N E S I S
  X   E   X   C   V   V   N
C O A L   T R A D E R O U T E
  T   I   I   R   N   L   R
Z I R C O N   B U S Q U E U E
  C   C   C   O   T   D   D
S A N D S T O N E   M I N E R
  I   D   T   I   O
O F U S E   A F T E R N O O N
  A   C   F   E   A   U
B I C O L O U R   R E L A T E
  E   V   S   O   L   A   C
U N D E R S T U D Y   Y O R E
  C   R   I   S   O   E   O
R E C Y C L E   E N T R O P Y
```

23

```
  H I T E C H   P R O P E R
  A   O   O   N   A   E   I
P R E P   M O O N S T R U C K
  R   E   M   R   C   D   K
F I D D L E   M E A L I E S T
  E   N   A   L   T   H
E R U D I T E L Y   N I N A
      E   I   O
  B A S H   A S T R O N O M Y
  A   C   I   A   E   I
C L A R I N E T   S A M O S A
  L   I   T   I   O   I   L
B A R B I E D O L L   R Y E S
  D   E   R   N   V   T   A
  S T R I N G   M E T H O D
```

24

```
  S A R T R E   A D O B E S
  A   A   E   C   I   A   H
E Y E D   G L O S S A R I E S
  W   I   A   U   O   B   B
P H W O A R   N E W S I T E M
  E       D   T   N   T   A
I N E L A S T I C   F O U R
      H       N       N
  S L A M   A G G R I E V E D
  C   S   P   S   E       T
M E G A L I T H   G I M L E T
  P   A   R   E   A   A   R
S T E P P A R E N T   K I N D
  I   S   T   P   T   E   A
  C O O P E R   B A R R E L
```

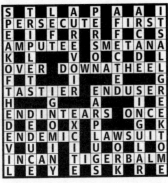

SOLUTIONS

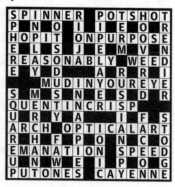

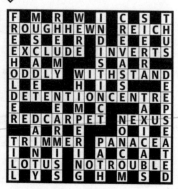

31

32

33

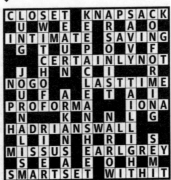

SOLUTIONS

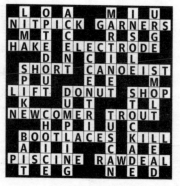

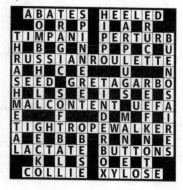

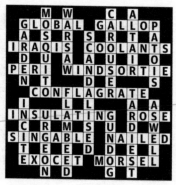

37

```
I N T O T H E B A R G A I N
N   H   R   C   U   A   R
V I O L A   O U T S M A R T
E   R   I   T   O   E   E   W
R U N I N T O   P E R U G I A
T   F   U   S       U   R
E X T R A   R O Y A L B L U E
B   E   R       O   A   H
R E L I E F M A P   C U R I O
A   L   A   O   A       U
T E A R F U L   T A L K E R S
E   P   E   W   H   C   L   E
  M A R I N A T E   A L B U M
    R   G   R   R   L   O   A
S T A N L E Y B A L D W I N
```

38

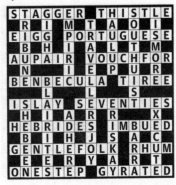

```
S T A G G E R   T H I S T L E
R   I   M   T   A   O   I
E I G G   P O R T U G U E S E
B   H   I   A   L   T   M
A U P A I R   V O U C H F O R
N   I   E   P   U   R
B E N B E C U L A   T I R E E
    L   L   L   S
I S L A Y   S E V E N T I E S
H   I   A   R   R   X
H E B R I D E S   I M B U E D
B   I   H   J   S   A   C
G E N T L E F O L K   R H U M
E   E   R   Y   A   R   T
O N E S T E P   G Y R A T E D
```

39

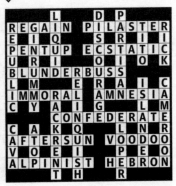

```
    L     D P
R E G A I N   P I L A S T E R
E   I   Q   S   R   I   I
P E N T U P   E C S T A T I C
U   R   I   O   I   O   K
B L U N D E R B U S S
L   M   E   R   A   I   C
I M M O R A L   A M N E S I A
C   Y   A   I   G   L   M
    C O N F E D E R A T E
C   A   K Q   L   N   R
A F T E R S U N   V O O D O O
V   O   E   I   P   E   O
A L P I N I S T   H E B R O N
    T   H       R
```

261

SOLUTIONS

43

```
C A R A P A C E   A P L O M B
O   I   R   O   H   U     L
C A S U A L L Y   M A N T R A
C   Q   N   L   R     R   C
Y O U N G M A N   E M B A R K
X   E   S   T   L   A   G   E
        D E B A U C H E R Y
T   C   D   R   C   Y   D   E
H U R R I C A N E S
O   O   V   L   R   D   O   I
U N S A I D   P A R A F F I N
G   S   S     T   M   L   C
H Y B R I D   P I N A F O R E
T   A   O     O   G   V   S
S P R I N G   I N D E C E N T
```

44

```
  B   E   S   A   R   S   N
S O U T H E R N   A P P R O X
  R   O   L   I   I   O   F
O D I N   L U M I N A R I E S
  E   E   A   B   T   A
F L O W E R   T R O U S E R S
  L   H   E   W   W
C O R I N T H   E S S E N C E
  S   R   C   A   L
D I E T R I C H   F A R O U T
  R   D   A   A   L   E
M I C R O N E S I A   R O L E
  S   I   G   I   R   A   E
W E E V I L   N E E D I E S T
  S   E   E   G   D   L   S
```

45

```
V   B   P   M   B   E   P   S
A E R O S P A C E   P H O N E
N   E   A   I   I   E   X
D A Z Z L E D   T A C I T L Y
A   H   M     I   A   I
L O N G S   B O T T L E C A P
I   E   E   U   L   O
S E V E N D E A D L Y S I N S
E     E   R   E   S   T
D I S L O D G E S   M O O L I
  U   P   A   I   L   L
R A N C H E R   B I R Y A N I
I   D   Y   D   R   A   T   O
F I R S T   E V E R G R E E N
T   Y   E   N   D   E   D   S
```

SOLUTIONS

46

```
S T R I P E   E P I D E M I C
P   O   L       R   I   A   L
O S A K A   B R I N G H O M E
N   D   T   A   M   I   R   V
D I S C O U R S E   T O I L E
A   I       N   M   A   S   R
I N D E F E A S I B L E
C   E   I   C   N   I   F   H
    B R I L L I A N T I N E
B   A   E   E   S   G   R   R
O U S E L   G A T E H O U S E
W   L   I   O   E   E   R   F
W R O N G D O E R   L L A N O
O   P   H   S       L   N   R
W R E S T L E D   R O U T E D
```

47

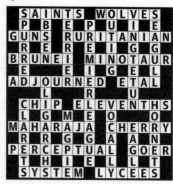

```
    S A I N T S   W O L V E S
    P   B   E   P   U   I   E
G U N S   R U R I T A N I A N
R   E   R   E   I   G   G
B R U N E I   M I N O T A U R
E       E   I   G   E   L
A D J O U R N E D   E T A L
    L       R       U
C H I P   E L E V E N T H S
L   G   M   E   O       O
M A H A R A J A   C H E R R Y
R   R   G   G   A   A   N
P E R C E P T U A L   G O E R
T   H   I   E   L   L   T
S Y S T E M   L Y C E E S
```

48

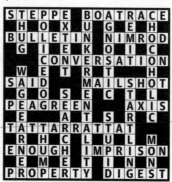

```
S T E P P E   B O A T R A C E
H   O   X   U   G   E   H
B U L L E T I N   N I M R O D
G   I   E   K   O   I   C
    C O N V E R S A T I O N
W   E   T   R   T       H
S A I D   M A I L S H O T
G   O   S   E   C   T   L
P E A G R E E N   A X I S
E       A   T   S   R   C
T A T T A R R A T T A T
R   H   C   L   U   L   M
E N O U G H   I M P R I S O N
E   M   E   T   I   N   N
P R O P E R T Y   D I G E S T
```

49

M	A		P		R	S		J		A		E
A	M	U	S	E	M	E	N	T		A	B	B	E	Y
N		S		R		C		A		N		R		R
S	I	T	E	S		T	I	T	L	E	P	A	G	E
		E		U		O		U		D				O
F	U	N	F	A	I	R		A	N	G	L	I	A	N
I			S			R		R		N		O		
E	N	V	O	I		S	H	Y		A	N	G	E	R
L		I		O		E		N						T
D	R	A	W	N	I	N		C	A	D	D	I	S	H
			M			S		R		O		D		
P	R	E	J	U	D	I	C	E		P	R	I	D	E
A		D		R		B		A		E		O		M
R	U	I	N	G		L	I	T	E	R	A	T	I	M
K		A		E		E		E		A		S		A

50

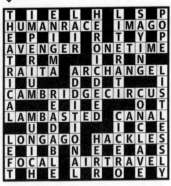

T		I	E	L		H		L	S		P
H	U	M	A	N	R	A	C	E		I	M	A	G	O
E		P		I		R		T		Y		P
A	V	E	N	G	E	R		O	N	E	T	I	M	E
T		R		M		I		R		N		
R	A	I	T	A		A	R	C	H	A	N	G	E	L
I		U		D		D		T				I
C	A	M	B	R	I	D	G	E	C	I	R	C	U	S
A			E		I				O			T
L	A	M	B	A	S	T	E	D		C	A	N	A	L
	U		D		I			I		I		C		E
L	O	N	G	A	G	O		H	A	C	K	L	E	S
E		I		B		N		E		E		A		S
F	O	C	A	L		A	I	R	T	R	A	V	E	L
T		H	E		L		R		O		E		Y

51

	S	P	O	I	L	E	R	A	L	E	R	T	
C		A		L		A		U		O		E	
L	O	U	R	D	E	S		B	E	S	I	D	E	S
A		S		B		T		L		T		L		E
S	T	A	T	I	N	S		E	G	O	T	I	S	M
S		G		L		T		U		N		I		
W	H	E	E	L		R	O	A	S	T	B	E	E	F
A				A		S								I
R	I	G	H	T	A	W	A	Y		B	I	S	O	N
F		O		I		O		E		A		A		
A	D	O	P	T	E	D		U	N	E	Q	U	A	L
R		D		B		R		W		G		C		I
E	B	B	T	I	D	E		E	Y	E	L	I	D	S
		Y		T		A		R		E		E		T
	W	E	L	S	H	D	R	E	S	S	E	R	

SOLUTIONS

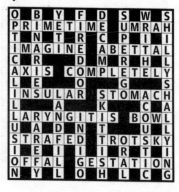

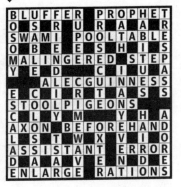

```
B L U F F E R   P R O P H E T
O   S   R   U   R   A   A   R
S W A M I   P O O L T A B L E
O   B   E   E   S   H   I   S
M A L I N G E R E D   S T E P
Y   E   D   C   I   U   A
    A L E C G U I N N E S S
E   C   I   R   T   A   S   S
S T O O L P I G E O N S
C   L   Y   M   Y   H   A
A X O N   B E F O R E H A N D
L   S   T   W   X   V   I   O
A S S I S T A N T   E R R O R
D   A   A   V   E   N   D   E
E N L A R G E   R A T I O N S
```

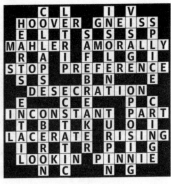

```
    C   L       I   V
H O O V E R   G N E I S S
E   L   T   S   S   S   P
M A H L E R   A M O R A L L Y
R   A   I   F   L   G   I
S T O P   P R E F E R E N C E
S   S       B   N       E
    D E S E C R A T I O N
E       C   E       P   C
I N C O N S T A N T   P A R T
T   B   T   K   U   O   I
L A C E R A T E   R I S I N G
I   R   T   R   P   I   G
L O O K I N   P I N N I E
    N   C       N   G
```

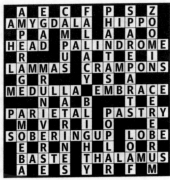

```
A   E   C   F   P   S   Z
A M Y G D A L A   H I P P O
P   A   M   L   A   A   O
H E A D   P A L I N D R O M E
R   U   A   T   E   I
L A M M A S   C R A M P O N S
G   R   Y   S   A
M E D U L L A   E M B R A C E
N   A   B   T   E
P A R I E T A L   P A S T R Y
M   V   R   I   O   E
S O B E R I N G U P   L O B E
E   R   N   H   L   O   R
B A S T E   T H A L A M U S
A   E   S   Y   R   F   M
```

SOLUTIONS

58

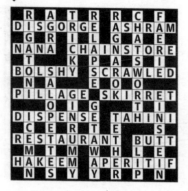

R		A		T		R		R	C		F
D	I	S	G	O	R	G	E		A	S	H	R	A	M
G		R		I		L		G		A		E
N	A	N	A		C	H	A	I	N	S	T	O	R	E
T		K		P		A		S		S		I
B	O	L	S	H	Y		S	C	R	A	W	L	E	D
N		A		E		O		O		R			
P	I	L	L	A	G	E		S	K	I	R	R	E	T
		O		I		G		T				I
D	I	S	P	E	N	S	E		T	A	H	I	N	I
C		E		R		T		E				S
R	E	S	T	A	U	R	A	N	T		B	U	T	T
M		T		M		W		H		L		E
H	A	K	E	E	M		A	P	E	R	I	T	I	F
N		S		Y		Y		R		P		N

59

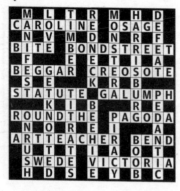

M		L		T		R		M		H		D
C	A	R	O	L	I	N	E		O	S	A	G	E
N		V		M		D		N		R		F
B	I	T	E		B	O	N	D	S	T	R	E	E	T
F				E		E		T		I		A
B	E	G	G	A	R		C	R	E	O	S	O	T	E
S		E				K		R		B		
S	T	A	T	U	T	E		G	A	L	U	M	P	H
		K		I		B				R		E
R	O	U	N	D	T	H	E		P	A	G	O	D	A
N		O		R		E		I		A		A
A	R	T	T	E	A	C	H	E	R		B	E	N	D
U				T		T		I		O		T
S	W	E	D	E		V	I	C	T	O	R	I	A
H		D		S		E		Y		B		C

60

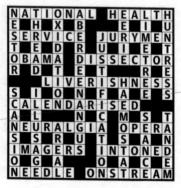

N	A	T	I	O	N	A	L		H	E	A	L	T	H
E		H		X		B				E		I		U
S	E	R	V	I	C	E		J	U	R	Y	M	E	N
T		E		D		R		U		I		E		T
O	B	A	M	A		D	I	S	S	E	C	T	O	R
R		D		T		E		T				R		E
		L	I	V	E	R	I	S	H	N	E	S	S
S		I		O		N		F		A		E		S
C	A	L	E	N	D	A	R	I	S	E	D
A		L		N		C		M		S		T
N	E	U	R	A	L	G	I	A		O	P	E	R	A
S		S		R		U		T		S		A		N
I	M	A	G	E	R	S		I	N	T	O	N	E	D
O		G		A				O		A		C		E
N	E	E	D	L	E		O	N	S	T	R	E	A	M

61

```
B R E A K I N   S P A R E D
L   N E   O   R E   I
O D D M E N T S   M I S S U S
W   S   P E   H M   E   O
    S L E D G E H A M M E R
C   S E   I   L   B   D
O U T O F R A N G E   L I E
T   A   T   N H U   I R
T U G     S U S T E N A N C E
A   G   O B   D G D
G R E E N F I N C H E S
E   R   E S   H R B H
P A I N T S   V I C T O R I A
I   N W   L O I I
E G G N O G   D O W A G E R
```

62

```
S M I D G E O N   C E L L A R
U   L   I L   X E   U
P A L I S A D E   S T E A M S
E   U M M   M E   N   E
R E S T O R A T I O N
S   T   N N S   S S   D E
O G R E S   S U S P I C I O N
N   A T   B T O S D
I N T E R M E S H   N O B L E
C   E E   A   E   E A
    S C R A P D E A L E R
W P S   D   O X   I M
A D R I F T   D I S C R E T E
R   A U   N   E V N
M A Y F L Y   S T I L L E S T
```

63

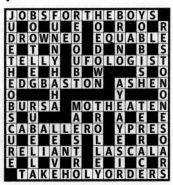

```
J O B S F O R T H E B O Y S
U   O   U E   O R O   R
D R O W N E D   E Q U A B L E
E   T   N O D N B   S
T E L L Y   U F O L O G I S T
H   E   H   B W   S   O
E D G B A S T O N   A S H E N
O   H   Y   O
B U R S A   M O T H E A T E N
S   U   A R   A E   E
C A B A L L E R O   Y P R E S
U   E E S   L E   R   O
R E L I A N T   L A S C A L A
E   L   V   R E   I C   R
  T A K E H O L Y O R D E R S
```

SOLUTIONS

64

```
M F S I N   P F E
A T A G L A N C E   A V O I D
D   I   A K   W   T   R   D
A E R A T E S   B E R G M A N
G   Y   E     E   I   E
A D D E R   I N D E C O R U M
S   O   N   F   I     A
C O M P A S S I O N A T E L Y
A   R   R   O   R     M M
R O C K S O L I D   H I P P O
  R   O   V     A H   R
B E Y O N C E   B A R G A I N
A   I   I N   Y   A S   I
D I N E S   C H R I S T I A N
E   G T   Y   D S   S   G
```

65

```
R O O T B O U N D   C Y A N
O   B   L   P   E   O   W
D Y E S T U F F   P O W D E R
A   C   E   R   R   B   S
U L C E R S   O V E R A C T S
  N     S   N   S   N   R
A T H E N A   T A S T E F U L
U   X     E   E     C
P R U S S I A N   D E C O K E
Q   U   O   O     R
S U P R E M E S   V I O L E T
O   R   A   T   I   W   Y
S I L E N T   R E C E N T R E
  S   A   I   U   A   E   I
T E A L   C A M B R I D G E
```

66

```
B A R A B R I T H   R I P E
E   A   R   C   A   E   I
T A B U L A T E   R U B E N S
C   N   G   B   B   E   T
C H A C H A   E X O R C I S E
  H     R   U   C   I
S T A Y U P   G A R B A N Z O
H   U       E     E
L I B E L L E D   D R E A D S
G   M   L   E   N
T H E I D I O T   N U D I S T
B   R   T   R   A   O   H
M O N A C O   A B N O R M A L
N   T   F   I   N   S   F
M E M E   F U N D A M E N T
```

67

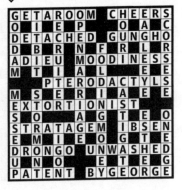

```
G E T A R O O M ■ C H E E R S
O ■ I ■ E ■ P ■ O ■ A ■ C
D E T A C H E D ■ G U N G H O
D ■ B ■ R ■ N ■ F ■ R ■ L ■ R
A D I E U ■ M O O D I N E S S
M ■ T ■ I ■ A ■ L ■ E ■ E ■ S
■ ■ P T E R O D A C T Y L S ■
M ■ S ■ E ■ R ■ I ■ A ■ E ■ E
E X T O R T I O N I S T ■ ■ ■
S ■ O ■ ■ A ■ G ■ T ■ E ■ O
S T R A T A G E M ■ I B S E N
E ■ M ■ I ■ E ■ O ■ G ■ T ■ E
D R O N G O ■ U N W A S H E D
U ■ N ■ O ■ ■ E ■ T ■ E ■ G
P A T E N T ■ B Y G E O R G E
```

68

```
F R E I G H T ■ S U N D O W N
■ A ■ M ■ U ■ T ■ S ■ E ■ O
I C E M A N ■ O V E R A L L S
■ C ■ I ■ G U N ■ F ■ N ■ F
C O U G A R ■ G R U E S O M E
■ O ■ R ■ Y ■ U ■ L ■ ■ A
S N E A K ■ W E L L S P E N T
■ ■ T ■ B ■ T ■ Y ■ R ■ ■ ■
H O M E B R E W S ■ G O O S E
■ A ■ ■ O ■ I ■ I ■ C ■ T
C R E V I C E S ■ M E R L I N
■ F ■ I ■ C ■ T O P ■ E ■ N
D I S P R O V E ■ O R A N G E
■ S ■ E ■ L ■ R ■ S ■ N ■ E
C H A R L I E ■ J E S T E R S
```

69

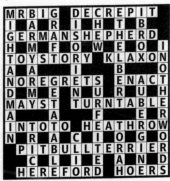

```
M R B I G ■ D E C R E P I T
I ■ A ■ R ■ I ■ H ■ T ■ B
G E R M A N S H E P H E R D
H ■ M ■ F ■ O ■ W ■ E ■ O ■ I
T O Y S T O R Y ■ K L A X O N
A ■ A ■ ■ I ■ ■ B ■ ■ O
N O R E G R E T S ■ E N A C T
D ■ M ■ E ■ N ■ U ■ R ■ U ■ H
M A Y S T ■ T U R N T A B L E
A ■ ■ A ■ ■ F ■ ■ E ■ R
I N T O T O ■ H E A T H R O W
N ■ R ■ A ■ C ■ I ■ O ■ G ■ O
■ P I T B U L L T E R R I E R
■ ■ C ■ L ■ I ■ E ■ A ■ N ■ D
H E R E F O R D ■ H O E R S
```

SOLUTIONS

70

71

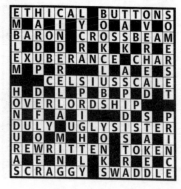

72

73

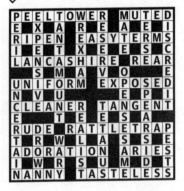

74

75

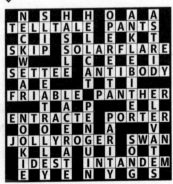

SOLUTIONS

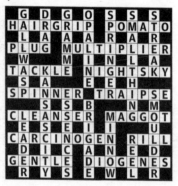

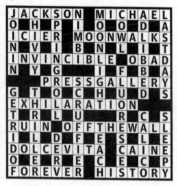

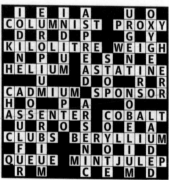

79

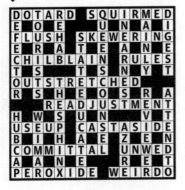

80

81

SOLUTIONS

82

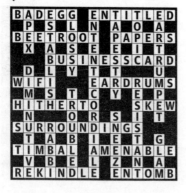

```
BADEGG   ENTITLED
 P  S  L  N  A O  A
BEETROOT   PAPERS
 X  A  S  E  E  I  T
    BUSINESSCARD
 D  L  Y  T  T     U
WIFI    EARDRUMS
 M  S  T  C  Y  E  P
HITHERTO     SKEW
 N     O  R  S  I  T
SURROUNDINGS
 T  A  B  I  E  T  G
TIMBAL   AMENABLE
 V  B  E  L  Z  N  A
REKINDLE   ENTOMB
```

83

```
FINGERS   DIAGRAM
 O  E  A  H  O  S  U  A
NEVER  ANDTHUMBS
 D  A  T  K  G  Y  M  S
LEDERHOSEN   FILE
 E  A  U     M  T  E  U
    MANICURISTS
 S  T  P  A  A  O  T  E
CHOLESTEROL
 R  U  T  H     L  O  A
ARCH  LAWNTENNIS
 P  H  F  N  O  Y  H  Y
PRICELIST   BEALL
 E  N  L  E  C  U  N  U
DIGITAL   HASIDIM
```

84

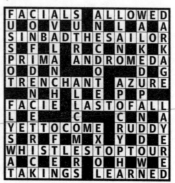

```
FACIALS   ALLOWED
 U  O  V  U  N  L  A  A
SINBADTHESAILOR
 S  F  L  R  C  N  K  K
PRIMA   ANDROMEDA
 O  D  N     O     D  G
TRENCHANT  AZURE
 N  H  L  E  P  P  E
FACIE  LASTOFALL
 L  E     C     C  N  A
YETTOCOME  RUDDY
 S  R  F  M  X  Y  D  E
WHISTLESTOPTOUR
 A  C  E  R  O  H  W  E
TAKINGS   LEARNED
```

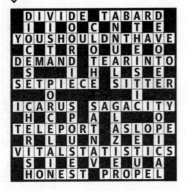

SOLUTIONS

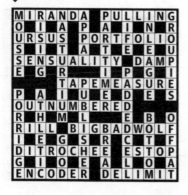

88

```
M I R A N D A   P U L L I N G
O   I   A   P   A   I   N   R
U R S U S   P O R T F O L I O
S   I   T   A   T   E   E   U
S E N S U A L I T Y   D A M P
E   G   R       I P G   I
    T A P E M E A S U R E
P A   I   U   E D   E   S
O U T N U M B E R E D
R   H   M   L       E   B   O
R I L L   B I G B A D W O L F
I   E   G   S R   C   T   F
D I T R O C H E E   E S T O P
G   I   O   E A L   O   A
E N C O D E R   D E L I M I T
```

89

```
H Y P E D U P   P O R K P I E
I   I   U   O   U   A   E   X
J U L E P   L I B E R T I N E
A   A   L   K   L   E   G   M
C I T R I C A C I D   S N A P
K   E   C       C   S   O   T
      L A B Y R I N T H I N E
O   I   T   A   S   R   R   D
C O N S E C R A T I O N
C   T   S   D       K   G   S
L Y E S   A S Y M M E T R I C
U   R   P   T   I   P   E   R
D E M E A N I N G   L I E G E
E   I   P   C   H   A   N   E
S E T B A C K   T R Y P S I N
```

90

```
P U B L I C R E L A T I O N S
E   A   L   A   I   U   I   P
N O N P L U S   G O R I L L A
I   A   U   T   H   B   S   C
S U N   S M A R T C O O K I E
T   A   O       Y   T   I
O B S T R U C T E D   S N O W
N   Y   R   A   B       O
E T C H   R E C R E A T I O N
    L   C   E       S   R   D
A S I T H A P P E N S   A G E
R   M   E   I   M   D   N   R
E M B R A C E   C A R D I F F
N   E   P   S   E   U   A   U
A I R P O R T T E R M I N A L
```

91

92

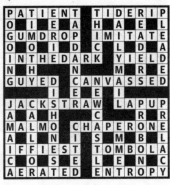

93

SOLUTIONS

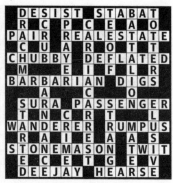

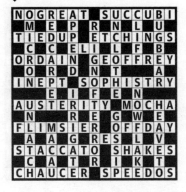

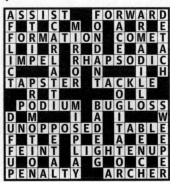

SOLUTIONS

100

```
S P A N I S H A R M A D A
D   O   O   N   C   I   U   G
U N I T T R U S T   S I N G E
T   S   E   G   R   I   N   R
C R O W D   G R E E N R O O M
H   N   L   S   F   A
A N I M A T E   S T O L L E N
U   N   L   R   A   M
C O G N A T E   D E M E S N E
T   R   V   R   S   A
I N C O M M O D E   G R I T S
O   R   B   L   S   R   T   L
N I O B E   V E S T I B U L E
S   W   L   E   E   S   D   S
  E N G L I S H S E T T E R
```

101

```
A B S O R B S   V E R A N D A
  L   R   R   R   G   N   R
H E R A   I C E B R E A K E R
  W   T   S   I   E   R   S
D I R E C T   N O T E C A S E
  T   O   C   S   H   E
A S H M O L E A N   F I O R D
  A   R   R   S
S C O R E   I N T H E M A I N
  H   G   B   A   A   G
M O R A L I S T   B A T O N S
  P   R   A   I   I   A   O
S P O I L S P O R T   S A R K
  E   N   E   N   A   T   E
F R I E N D S   A T T E N D S
```

102

```
B   F   W   S   H   P   M   A
A U R E I   P H Y S I C I A N
T   A   F   L   S   S   L   T
H I N D E R E R S   T A L E S
  K   N   O   O   E
P O L I C E D   P I L G R I M
I   I   A   I   G   O
C A N O N   D I P   R I P E N
O   T   R   I   A   K
T O P G E A R   I M P A R T S
  R   R   E   O   D
C L I M B   E A R T H H O G S
O   E   U   V   E   O   N   A
O B S E R V E R S   C L E R K
K   T   Y   S   S   K   R   E
```

```
S I D E M A N   P I L E S U P
K   I   O   A   R I   T   A
O N S E T   P O O H P O O H S
P   O   O   P   P S   T   S
J A W B R E A K E R   T I C K
E   N   M   L   S   N   E
    T O N S I L H O C K E Y
S   D   U   U   E   R   A S
P O I N T O F O R D E R
A   S   H   F     T   R   S
N E C K   S O N G T H R U S H
K   L   T   C   E   R   B T
I N A N I M A T E   O M B R E
N   I   C   T   S   A   E T
G U M S H O E   E N T H R A L
```

```
B   A   P   H   S H   G   M
R A T I O N A L E   A D E L E
O   R   T   I   R   L   M S
T R O T T E R   A F F A I R S
H   O   Y   I   P   A N   A
E X P O   B E D H O P P I N G
L   E   S   S     I   E
C U R R E N T   S E N A T O R
R   V   H   T     I   E
E X P R E S S I O N   M A R C
E   O   N   A   R   S M   E
P I L O T E D   T I M P A N I
E   L   E   I   L   A R   V
R E E V E   S W E A R L I K E
S   X   N   T   G T   A   D
```

```
V E N I C E   S P R O U T
A   I   L   I   U V   I
E G G S   A N N U L M E N T S
R   E   N   A   L R   A
R A T I N G   P A I N T I N G
N   E   P   N   A   I
I T I N E R A R Y   E X E C
    O   O   E
M O D E   S P O R T S C A R
O   U   N   R   E   C
K O H L R A B I   S T E W E D
R   A   R   A   I   N   T
P A S T O R A T E S   E D A M
G   E   O   E   T   M   T
E N D O W S   E S C A P E
```

SOLUTIONS

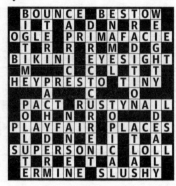

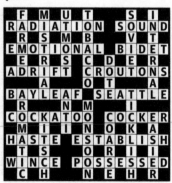

Puzzle 109:

W	G	C	C	G	I	A	J
A	P	R	I	L	F	O	O	L		C	A	L	V	E

Puzzle 110

Puzzle 111

SOLUTIONS

112

P	R	O	C	E	S	S		V	E	T	E	R	A	N
A		R		T		S		G		P		N		
F	I	V	E		I	N	T	E	R	D	I	C	T	S
L		D		C		I		E		C		W		
O	C	L	O	C	K		F	I	S	S	U	R	E	S
A			L		F		S		R			R		
T	R	U	M	P	E	D	U	P		K	E	E	P	A
		O			P			A						
A	C	T	U	P		S	P	I	K	E	N	A	R	D
A		N		I		E		A				H		
O	L	D	T	I	M	E	R		S	H	A	D	O	W
D		A		P		L		H		B		N		
T	E	P	I	D	A	R	I	U	M		B	A	C	K
R		N		L		P		I		O		H		
P	A	I	S	L	E	Y		W	R	I	T	E	I	N

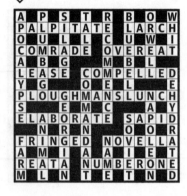

113

A		P		S		T		R		B		O		W
P	A	L	P	I	T	A	T	E		L	A	R	C	H
O		U		L		L		C		U		W		I
C	O	M	R	A	D	E		O	V	E	R	E	A	T
A		B		G				M		B		L		
L	E	A	S	E		C	O	M	P	E	L	L	E	D
Y		G			O		E		L					E
P	L	O	U	G	H	M	A	N	S	L	U	N	C	H
S				E		C				A				Y
E	L	A	B	O	R	A	T	E		S	A	P	I	D
		N		R		N		O		O		R		
F	R	I	N	G	E	D		N	O	V	E	L	L	A
A		M		I		A		I		E		I		
R	E	A	T	A		N	U	M	B	E	R	O	N	E
M		L		N		T		E		T		N		D

114

	P	H	O	T	O	F	I	N	I	S	H	
I		A		P		C		M		N		A		A
C	E	L	L	I	S	T		P	Y	R	A	M	I	D
E		A		N		O		E		U		M		W
B	E	E	K	E	E	P	E	R		S	H	E	B	A
A		O			O		I		H		R		R
G	E	N	T		A	D	U	L	T	E	R	A	T	E
	T		F						S		N		
S	P	O	I	L	S	P	O	R	T		E	D	I	T
A		L		A		I		E			S		W
B	R	O	O	M		T	R	A	N	S	P	I	R	E
I		G		B		F		L		E		C		E
C	H	I	M	E	R	A		I	N	V	O	K	E	D
U		S		A		L		S	E	L		Y
	T	O	U	T	L	E	M	O	N	D	E	